Insuring Tomorrow

Engaging Millennials in the Insurance Industry

By Tony Cañas, CPCU, MBA and Carly Burnham, CPCU, MBA

Ordering Information:
Quantity sales. Special discounts might be available on quantity purchases, reach out by email.

Table of Contents

Dedication

To my parents, Bernadette and Jess Burnham, who continually encourage me in creating a career I love.

To my sister, Meghan Burnham, who serves as a sounding board and advisor for all of my ideas and goals.

To my husband, Andrew Kamps, for truly being my partner and supporting me in all of my endeavors.

Carly

~~~

To my mom, Dr. Marlene Jiménez, who taught me the value of hard work and finding a career I loved.

To my dad, Tony Cañas III, who infused in me his love of the business world.

To my life-partner, Renee Bruns, for putting up with my obsession with the insurance industry, and for finally pushing me to put it all down on paper.

Tony

Introduction

"For years, the insurance industry has failed to engage enough professionals to help bridge the growing skills gap resulting from impending retirements. Now, the mass talent shortage is here and insurers must take action."

- Gregory P. Jacobson, Co-CEO of Jacobson Group[1].

The President of the National CPCU Society opened the 2012 conference by saying, "My predecessor last year opened this conference announcing that we have a looming demographic crisis. That announcement had been made for a few years by his predecessors. Today I'm here to tell you that we no longer have a *looming* demographic crisis. We have a demographic crisis, period. It's no longer looming, it's here."

He proceeded to ask the group, around 350 people, to raise their hand if they were under 30. I was one of around ten people to raise their hand. I came back the next year and the same question was asked. This time only about eight of us raised our hands.

That first CPCU Society Leadership summit in 2012 started me on what would become more than five-year-long obsession with Millennials in the Insurance Industry. When I got home, I dug into the topic with a vengeance, reading everything that I could find

---

[1] 2016 Insurance Industry Talent Trends

about Millennial employees and trying to understand why our wonderful industry has such a hard time engaging Millennials. This book is the natural culmination of all that work.

My obsession led me to connect with the Nationwide Gen Y Associate Resource Group, which at the time only existed at Nationwide's headquarters in Columbus, Ohio. I started a new chapter of the group in Nationwide's second-biggest office, Des Moines, Iowa.

The Gen Y group led me to meet Carly and to become active in Yammer, Nationwide's in-house social network. We used Yammer to reach out to other Millennials at Nationwide all over the country and helped them figure out how to grow in our industry. We continued to help run and grow the Gen Y group until Carly and I departed from Nationwide.

After leaving Nationwide, we both missed the platform that the Gen Y group and Yammer had given us to make a difference. We decided to expand our efforts to the overall industry and started blogging, first on LinkedIn's Pulse platform and a couple of months later on our own platform - InsNerds.com.

Two years after the conference in Fort Lauderdale, I was invited to present about retaining Millennials in the industry at the 2014 CPCU Leadership Summit, the very same conference that had originally gotten me hooked on the topic, and later that year at the 2014 CPCU Society Annual Meeting in Anaheim, California. Since then I've presented my session on Millennials at a variety of industry conferences three to four times a year.

We decided to organize this book by mirroring the order of my presentation. Chapters 1-3 will help you understand Millennials and why the insurance industry is having trouble retaining them. Chapters 5-13 provide tactical solutions to the problem that MUST be implemented if we want to be successful. They're the table stakes. If we can't figure out how to do those, we have very little chance to engage Millennials in insurance. Chapters 15-28 dive into the more difficult changes that would help make the industry a truly amazing industry to work in, and are more strategic solutions. These are more advanced concepts. They're not absolutely necessary, but picking some can really help your company stand out. Chapter 25 takes a quick look at what's coming after the Millennials and gives you an introduction to Generation Z, who are starting to trickle into the industry. Finally, Chapter 26 gives you a view into what we need to do to become a talent factory for our industry.

"Above all, it is a call to action. The one thing leaders cannot do is nothing. They cannot wait for trends to pass them by, and they cannot wait for Millennials to get older and start behaving like

Baby Boomers. That won't happen. This workforce isn't going to acclimate to the status quo."[2]

- From the 2017 State of the American Workforce report by Gallup

We are truly passionate about making the insurance industry the best industry out there. I really hope you enjoy the book!

Sincerely,

Tony Cañas, CPCU, MBA, ARM, ARe, ASLI, AIC, API, AMIM
Chief Motivator
InsNerds.com

---

[2] The State of the American Workforce - Gallup 2017 - p. 8

Chapter 1: An Industry in Demographic Crisis

"Insurance companies need to solve the predicted 25% of workplace retirements in the next four years."
-2017 Insurance Industry Employment and Hiring Outlook Survey by GreatInsuranceJobs.com

Since early 2015, Millennials are already the largest generation in the workforce, and the proportion that they make up will only keep growing as Baby Boomers transition into retirement. In fact, by 2020, they will be 50%; and by 2025, 75% of all employees in the workforce will be Millennials. In insurance, this transformation will be harder than in most industries since Boomers are overrepresented compared to the overall labor force.

Many Boomers delayed retirement after the Great Recession in 2008 because their 401(k)s took a big hit. But as we prepare to go to press with this book in early 2017, the stock market stands at new record highs. This means that not only are 65 year olds retiring, but the 66 to 70 year olds who stayed in the labor force longer than they had planned are finally able to retire. This is causing a massive wave of retirements hitting the industry. This is probably easily visible in your office where chances are you see a lot of retirement parties. In the small 200 person office where Tony works in Atlanta, Georgia, he has seen three anniversary celebrations for people with over 30 years of service in just the last six months.

The US Department of Labor estimates that between the wave of retirements and the expected growth of the business, our insurance industry will need to fill 400,000 positions in the next ten years. That's a lot of new Millennials coming into the industry! Good job (and thank you for) buying this book to get ahead of it. We've been immersed in this topic for at least the last five years and will do our best to help you understand it.

The average age of an insurance professional in the United States today is around 60 years old, and the number of insurance professionals over 55 has increased by 74% in the decade before 2012, compared to only 45% in the overall workforce[3]. In fact, insurers have more exposure to the aging workforce than most industries. Today, only about 25% of the insurance workforce is under 35 years old[4]. This presents a major demographic crisis to the industry that we have seen coming for several years, but that we have thus far been unable to solve.

To understand this phenomenon, we first need to understand the demographics of the US workforce and how it is changing.

[3] McKinsey & Company: Building a Talent Magnet - How the Property and Casualty Insurance Industry Can Solve Its People Needs 2010
[4] Solving the Insurance Talent Crisis by Investing in RMI Graduates - IRMI Sept 2015

Demographers disagree on the actual beginning and end of each generation, but for the purposes of this book we will use the following years:

Generation	Born	Population
Baby Boomer	1946 - 1964	80 million
Gen X	1965 - 1976	60 million
Gen Y/Millennials	1977 - 1995	80 million

The most important thing to realize about these generations is that both Baby Boomers, born after the return of the troops from World War II, and Millennials consist of around 80 million people. These figures make both of these generations 20 million people (25%) larger than Gen X, which is sandwiched in between them. Millennials (or Gen Y) have also been called Echo Boomers because they are literally the kids of Baby Boomers.

According to the Council of Economic Advisers, by 2014, Millennials were already the largest and most diverse generation in the US. In that same year, the share of 20 to 34 year olds born abroad was 15%, much higher than it was any time in the previous 50 years, and near the high of 20% in 1910 (during the previous large wave of immigration). A record 42% of individuals identify with a race or ethnicity other than white. The share of Hispanics alone in this age group tripled between 1980 and 2012 from 7% to 21%.

By the year 2000, Millennials made up 6% of the workforce while Boomers made up 48%. As more Millennials graduated college, and more Boomers started retiring, those numbers started to reverse. By 2015, Millennials made up 35% of the workforce and Boomers only 31%. Obviously the numbers will only keep moving in the same direction. The smaller Gen X generation has stayed flat at around 32% of the workforce over the last 15 years as they are neither new to the workforce nor quite at the point in their careers where they're likely to retire[5]. By 2025, three out of four workers will be Millennials[6].

So going back to insurance, historically, almost nobody grew up wanting to work in insurance (unless their dad was an agent, and often those kids chose not to follow in dad's footsteps). In fact, research has found that only 4% of Millennials are interested in a career in insurance[7]. This is partially because the industry has a bad reputation, and partially because there are very few Risk Management and Insurance (RMI) programs in colleges and universities. Those programs are awesome but they only exist at around 70 of the 3,000+ schools in the country and only feed 15% of our new talent needs each year. A full 85% of our new hires come without any sort of insurance background!

---

[5] Bureau of Labor Statistics: https://www.bls.gov/
[6] https://www.bdcnetwork.com/workplace-design-trends-make-way-millennials
[7] The Hartford - A Generation of Leaders

McKinsey & Company's 2010 report *Building a Talent Magnet - How the Property and Casualty Insurance Industry Can Solve Its People Needs* identified three major challenges for our industry to attract high quality young talent:

1. Poor reputation
2. Limited understanding among high school and college students of the industry's career opportunities
3. Limited pool of trained talent

The same report found that as Baby Boomers retire, every industry will be affected but **insurance will be affected even more because the proportion of workers 55 and older is 30% higher than in the rest of economy.**

A survey of Ohio students by the Ohio Insurance Institute in 2011 found that the majority of the students knew someone working in the industry. But, more than 40% were uninterested in working in insurance or even learning about insurance careers. This tells us that we are partially at fault! We are not being communicative enough about how awesome the industry is for a long-term career. We have met so many people who have worked in the industry for many years and love it, but they're not telling their kids and their friends' kids the good things. We need to stop apologizing for working in insurance, and get proud and loud! Most of the students in the survey understood that the industry is important and that we have a variety of careers, but nevertheless perceived us as boring. That's not all - less than two of five adults in the US felt positively about insurance in a 2008 survey by the Reputation Institute, and none of the 11 major US carriers were perceived positively. Yikes!

The numbers are worse than most of us could even imagine. Only 2% of recent college grads are interested in working for an insurance company[8].

The LinkedIn Top Companies 2017 rankings, which measure where people want to work based on their analytics of job applications, engagement, and employee retention as reported to employees found that not a single insurance company broke into the top 50[9]. We are seeing some improvement in the Fortune Top Places to Work 2017 where both Nationwide and USAA made it into the top 100!

The public thinks of the industry as "stagnant, outdated, and not providing a public service," and some of the big carriers and brokers are perceived as "conservative, boring, and not innovative." Many Millennials report thinking of a job in the industry as 'rigid and slow paced[10].'

---

[8] Accenture - The Insurance Workforce of the Future
[9] https://www.linkedin.com/pulse/behind-linkedin-top-companies-2017-daniel-roth?published=t
[10] Deloitte: Generational Talent Management for Insurers

In 2016, Gallup found that in the overall economy, only half of Millennials are planning to be at the same company at this time next year. Only 10% said they expected to be in their current job in two years compared to 41% of Boomers[11].

Almost all of us fell into insurance by accident, and we stayed because of loyalty, and because we found a rewarding and fulfilling career. The problem is that Millennials are not as loyal as previous generations (or more accurately, as we'll explain further in later chapters, they see loyalty in a different way), and as an industry, we are having a very hard time retaining, engaging, and growing them. Every year, large insurance carriers hire thousands of freshly minted college graduates, only to lose many of them two or three years later. We have thus far been unable to secure retention stats about Millennials in the industry, probably because companies are embarrassed to admit they have an issue. But the fact that the issue is discussed constantly in the insurance trade press and at insurance conferences, along with our own conversations with thousands of young insurance professionals over the past few years, has made us confident that as an industry we are churning through a lot of our young professionals.

---

[11] Gallup: There's no job Millennials won't leave.

Research by The Hartford has found that when Millennials are asked if they want to work in insurance only 4%[12] say they're interested! Ouch! We have done our own research by live-surveying Millennials in attendance when Tony gives his session on Retaining Millennials in the Insurance Industry at various conferences throughout the country. We asked them to tell us anonymously what they thought of the industry BEFORE somebody got them interested in working in it and dynamically generate a word cloud with their answers. The results usually yield something like this:

---

[12] The Hartford - A Generation of Leaders

By 2016, the average 2010-2014 graduate had already worked at three different employers, and only 29% of Millennials report feeling engaged at work[13]. So look around: Out of the young faces, only three out of ten are happy at work; the rest are probably job searching on their phones right now. And that's assuming insurance matches other industries. It could be that ours are even less engaged! On average, those who graduated college between 2006 and 2010 have worked at almost twice as many companies as those who graduated between 1986 and 1990.[14]

In the past year, 21% of Millennials reported changing jobs. This is three times the number of non-Millennials who changed employers. Some of this is normal for their stage of life, but the numbers are much higher compared to what they were when Boomers were the same age[15].

Needless to say, this is not the most encouraging way to start this book, but it paints a clear picture of reality. The sad reality is that Millennials think our industry is boring, and as we all know, perception is reality. If you ask people who have been working in the industry for a few years, pretty much all of them would describe it as anything but boring.

---

[13] Gallup: There's no job Millennials won't leave.
[14] https://blog.linkedin.com/2016/04/12/will-this-year_s-college-grads-job-hop-more-than-previous-grads
[15] Gallup How Millennials Want to Work and Live

Another critical point to understand from the McKinsey research is that Millennials who work a couple of years at an insurance company and decide to leave don't just leave the company, they leave the industry entirely! The solutions we'll talk about later in this book can't guarantee you'll be able to keep them in the company, but at the very least, they should help in keeping most of them in the industry.

Chapter 2: Understanding the Millennials' Background in Contrast to the Baby Boomers

"People ask Gallup, 'Are Millennials really that different?' The answer is yes, profoundly so. Millennials will change the world decisively more than any other generation."
-*Jim Clifton, CEO of Gallup*[16]

Now that we've explained the critical importance for retaining Millennials, let's take a look at why this generation is so different (and so confusing) compared to previous generations.

Like most things in life, it comes down to the way they were raised and what they lived through as children. Millennials were raised by Baby Boomers who had a very distinct parenting philosophy from the generation that raised them. The parents of Millennials wanted them to have it better and easier than they did. They worked hard to give them the things and the opportunities they never had, and they were helped by an unprecedented time of economic growth from 1970 to 2000. Generations raised in time of relative wealth have interesting characteristics, and Millennials are perfect examples of this.

---

[16] How Millennials Want to Work and Live 2016

Generational expert Cam Marston gave the Keynote at the National Association of Mutual Insurance Companies (NAMIC)'s 2016 Annual Meeting. He explained that every generation sees life and work colored by the historical context they grew up in. The events of September 11, 2001 led Baby Boomers, who raised most Millennials, to become Helicopter Parents. Gen Xers, who raised some of the youngest Millennials, became Drone Parents, which are a bit different; you don't see them hovering about, but when necessary, they drop down and create a firestorm to save their kids.

Marston's research also focuses on how affluent societies raise kids in different ways than non-affluent societies. Boomers were raised in an era of scarcity, while Millennials were raised in a time of prosperity and affluence. Kids raised in affluent societies are raised with an individualistic "what's in it for me" attitude. Affluent societies also cause delayed adulthood and extended lifetimes, both of which explain a lot about the way Millennials see the world.

Affluent societies tell their kids they are special; Boomers were never told that. In fact, "Do you think you're special?" was more of a put-down than a real question. Boomers were raised to fit in and keep quiet. Millennials were raised with the idea that they are special, unique, magical snowflakes destined to change the world.

Boomers were told by their parents to "go find a job." A couple of decades later Boomers told their Millennial children to "go find a job that makes you happy." This makes a big difference in how Millennials see their jobs and their expectations when they start their first job. They expect their job to make them happy! Unfortunately, the workplace was never designed to make employees happy.

Baby Boomers were raised in a world with sharp corners. When Boomers were born, most of them were carried home from the hospital in their mother's arms, while she sat in the front seat of a 1950's car with metal bumpers, a metal dashboard, no airbags, and no seat belts. If their parents really loved them, they rolled down the window while they smoked! It was just a different, more innocent world. As children, they were sent outside to play in an innocent world blissfully unaware of the dangers that could befall them.

By the time Boomers had their own Millennial babies in the 1980s and 1990s, the world had changed. When Tony was ten years old, he asked for a skateboard for Christmas. His mom, the sometimes overprotective Dr. Marlene Jiménez, gave in, and he got his skateboard, along with a very strict rule that he was only to use it under adult supervision and while wearing a giant helmet, giant plastic knee pads, and giant elbow pads. We're not talking sporty knee pads, we're talking big cartoony ones. He couldn't have hurt himself if he tried! Just like most of his generational cohorts, Tony was raised in a world of padded corners and (often) overprotective parents.

With the hope of increasing their kids' chances of getting into the best universities, Boomer parents encouraged their Millennial children to participate in a large variety of extracurriculars from soccer to debate club, and the minivan became the symbol of the suburban mom. This left little time for the Millennials to take part time jobs like previous generations of Americans had.

Millennials grew up with a constant cadre of school counselors, teachers, coaches, and their parents protecting them and advising them. Those well meaning adults were largely believers in the self-esteem movement, and they often told kids they were special, protected their feelings, and coddled them. Schools stopped keeping score during baseball games, and many Millennials were awarded 19th place ribbons after undistinguished athletic performances. But hey, no feelings were hurt!

When Boomers were growing up, kids were expected to be seen and not heard, and when dad called you into his office, it was usually to tell you that you were in trouble. Boomers learned that if they kept their head down and did things correctly, they'd be rewarded, and no news was good news. Then they proceeded to raise their Millennial children the exact opposite way, giving them constant feedback and asking for their opinion. Millennials grew to need feedback and to believe that no feedback was bad news, which of course created communication issues with their Boomer bosses!

We are big fans of Jason Dorsey - "The Gen Y Guy" - and his books and research at the Center for Generational Kinetics. Many of the topics we'll talk about in this book come from his research; we just applied them to the insurance industry. As a matter of fact, we'd love to see Dorsey speak at a major insurance industry event! We highly recommend you read *Y Size Your Business* after you're done with this book for much more details on his ideas. We'll refer to his book often, so for brevity's sake from here on we'll just refer to it as *Y Size*.

In *Y Size*, Dorsey tells a story that really illustrates the difference between the two large generations in a better way than anything else we've found. We'll paraphrase it for you here, but nobody tells it like Dorsey, so we recommend you look it up on YouTube.

A Baby Boomer turns 18, and his parents meet him at the door. They're married, to each other. "John, we love you. We're so proud of you! But you're 18 now... So get another job, join the military, go to college, get married, we don't care. Just get out of here!" And 80 million Baby Boomers ran kicking and screaming into the world where they have been outworking the rest of us ever since.

A Millennial turns 18, and his parents meet him at the door. They made a special joint appearance for the occasion since they are no longer married. "Tony, we love you. We're so proud of you! But you're 18 now... So as long as you're going to college we'll help you out." And 80 million Millennials leisurely bought a new iPod and went off to college, some for a seven year associates degree. Now they've graduated and are coming to work for you! Are you ready?

(Nobody tells this story like Dorsey - you can watch him tell it on YouTube, so check it out there!)

Between 1973 and 2006 the cost of college skyrocketed while the career options to pursue with only a high school degree became more and more limited since more of the competition had college degrees. College became the new high school, while its cost increased to largely unaffordable levels. Unfortunately, the minimum wage didn't follow suit going from $1.60 per hour in 1973 to $5.15 per hour in 2006. Boomers were able to work during the summer and make enough to pay for a year of college, possibly earning enough to pay for room and board. Their Millennial children didn't have this option and were forced to borrow in record amounts. By 2014, student loan debt had ballooned to $1.3 trillion[17], and that number has only grown since.

Millennials are moving through life stages slower than previous generations did. In 2014, there were more adults living at home with their parents than with a spouse or significant other[18]. This is the first time this has happened in 130 years! Back in the 70s, the median Baby Boomer got married at 23 years old. Today, the median Millennial is getting married at age 30[19]. The percentage of 18 to 31 year old adults who are married and living on their own has declined from 56% in 1968 to 23% in 2012[20]. Among women, the percentage of 25 year olds who have children has dropped from 12.9% in the 1970s to 7.9% today[21]. The last time this many young Americans were living with a relative was in 1930, one year after the Great Depression[22].

Boomers and Millennials also have different views of employment in general. Boomers joined the working world with an expectation of lifetime employment, and for the most part, enjoyed a historic period of economic growth during the bulk of their working lives. Their theory of work was work hard, keep your head down, and

---

[17] http://www.federalreserve.gov/releases/g19/HIST/cc_hist_memo_levels.html
[18] Pew Research Center - Living with parents edges out other living arrangements
[19] Goldman Sachs- Report on Millennials
[20] Pew Research Center Current Population Survey
[21] IPUMS=CPS and Goldman Sachs Global Investment Research
[22] US Census 2015 Population Survey

you'll get rewarded. The company was supposed to take care of its people. Salary was the most important thing, and many Boomers lived to work. Boomers believed in powerful brand names and that working for a brand name company meant stability.

Millennials saw their parents and grandparents get downsized and lose their pensions. They entered the workforce as the first generation with no expectation of lifetime employment. Millennials are less brand loyal (both as consumers and as employees) and are more likely to see work as a means to an enjoyable lifestyle rather than as an end to itself. Millennials learned to value flexibility more than stability and even salary. Many of our Millennial friends would happily give up some salary in exchange for more vacation time, the ability to work from home, or to have more work life balance. The traditional 9 to 5 is just not a great match for Millennials. Seventy-seven percent say flexible hours would make the workplace more productive for them. It doesn't mean they want to work less, since 89% already check their work email after hours[23].

Every generation is marked by its relationship with technology based on which technologies were common during their formative years. Millennials were the first generation to (almost) not remember life before the Internet, and grew up with easily

---

[23] Bentley University - Mind of the Millennial

accessible computers in the classroom, at home, and by their teenage years, in their pockets.

A national survey of Human Resources professionals and of Millennial employees asked both groups whether Millennials are loyal at work. The great majority of the Millennials - 82% - answered that they are loyal at work. Of the HR professionals, only 1% agreed. This is a HUGE disconnect! What can possibly explain this?

Here's the key, and if you're going to remember one thing from this chapter, remember this - Millennials have a different definition of loyalty than previous generations did. For Boomers, loyalty means, "I came, I stayed 30 years, and I got my gold watch." For Millennials, loyalty means, "I worked very hard while I was there."

Tony is a perfect example of this. He has had seven jobs at four insurance carriers over the eight years he has been in the industry. From Tony's perspective, he is loyal. He worked hard in each and every one of those jobs. The problem is that he started in an entry level role, and if he wanted to make his dream of becoming an executive before turning 40 a reality, he needed to move fast!

The insurance industry has been lucky to have hundreds of thousands of insurance professionals who have been in the industry for 30-40 years, often at the same company! Millennials are very unlikely to do the same. The best we can hope is that they stay in the industry for the long-term, but not in the same company. We will have to change the way we manage our people to make the most out of such a dynamic workforce.

Ultimately, what it comes down to is that Millennials were raised in such a different way than previous generations that they are like a different culture, and not realizing this can cause endless aggravation for their Baby Boomer managers. After all, those darn kids grew up in the same country and speaking the same language. Why do they have to be so difficult!?

Millennials are basically a different culture. Think about it this way - if you had a Japanese business connection invite you to his home for dinner, would you be offended when he asked you to take your shoes off at the door? As long as you understood that this is simply a cultural difference, you probably would do it without delay and not think about it twice. It's the same concept with Millennials - you just need to understand that they're comparable to a different culture, and as such, they communicate differently.

Have you found yourself thinking, "They have to pay their dues!" Tony asks this question during his session on Millennials and generally gets a loud "Yes!" from the Boomers in the audience.

We completely understand. Boomers paid their dues when they started, quietly did the work, and didn't complain or ask for special treatment... and they made it! They made it big! We get it. But the industry has changed in ways you might not realize.

The quintessential entry level role in insurance for a brand new college graduate Boomer was something like a Multiline Claims Adjuster (maybe even in the field); a Personal Lines and Farm Underwriter; or if you were really lucky, the Allied School where kids were hired from all over the country and given an apartment in Des Moines, Iowa for a year while they were trained in insurance with the rest of the program members for a whole year. For half the year, they didn't even know whether they'd end up in claims or underwriting, they just got general training followed by specific training for their area.

Those jobs were truly awesome jobs where employees could actually show what they could do, and they could really pay their dues to get noticed. We are very envious! Those jobs, for the most part, don't exist anymore, or they are now middle level jobs that take a few years for a new graduate to qualify for them.

The quintessential entry level jobs Millennials find when they graduate college is much more likely to be a Call Center, Processing Center, or very specialized entry level claims role. Those jobs are very thin, could be easily done by a high school graduate, and usually get boring within a few months. They also offer little flexibility, low pay, and they make it VERY hard to "pay your dues."

By the time Millennials show up for orientation at their companies, they are the most educated generation ever with 47%[24] holding a postsecondary degree compared to only 29%[25] of Boomers. This is pretty well known. What is less well known is that they also have much less work experience and much less life experience. This is partially because their Boomer parents encouraged them to focus on extracurriculars instead of part time work during high school and college.

Millennials have less life experience than Boomers did at their age because they are graduating college later, marrying later, having kids later, buying a house later, and in urban (and even suburban) areas, many choose not to have a car and to walk, bike, or Uber/Lyft everywhere instead.

At college graduation age, Boomers were usually married, maybe even with a child already, and most were looking to buy their first homes. At 24 years old, most Boomers were adults!

---

[24] Council of Economic Advisors 2014
[25] https://www.55places.com/blog/10-interesting-baby-boomer-facts-stats

When researchers asked Millennials, "At what age does a kid become an adult?" their answer tends to come in at around **30 years old**. That's right. That 22 year old that you just hired right out of college doesn't even see him or herself as an adult, and won't for the next eight years!

Then there's also the question of what exactly constitutes a 'long-term' job. When Tony surveys attendees at conferences, Boomers tend to answer in the range of three to five years with some saying seven or even ten years. Research has found that Millennials think a job counts as long-term after only 11 months! So think about it - if we potentially only get them for 11 months before they're no longer afraid to change jobs, we *need* to get good at getting them trained and productive *as soon as possible*. Don't worry - we'll help you get them there!

While every generation has grown with advancing technology, Millennials have been defined by an exponential growth in the technology they have had available their whole lives. In 1980, IBM's first gigabyte hard drive weighed 550 lbs and cost $40,000. As we prepare to go to press in early 2017, the smallest hard drive for sale on Amazon is 20 GB and costs only $4.99. That's a 20 times upgrade on size for 1/8000th the price. The per gigabyte cost dropped from $40,000 per gigabyte to 25 cents.

When it comes to technology, the Council of Economic Advisers put it best in their 2014 report, "Millennials have come of age in a world in which the frontiers of technology have appeared unlimited."

And in a 2016 article published in The Atlantic titled *Can Millennials Undo What The Recession Did to Their Earnings,* "Millennials should, theoretically, be the highest-paid cohort of young adults in American history. They're the most educated group of workers and have entered the labor market at a time of high and increasing productivity. But thanks to a recession, a slow recovery, and staggering amounts of student debt, that hasn't happened."

The same article analyzes a study by the Center for American Progress titled *When I Was Your Age - Millennials and the Generational Wage Gap.* That research looked at the earnings of 30 year olds in 1984, 2004, and 2014 in inflation adjusted real terms. It found that a 30 year old today makes about the same as a 30 year old did in 1984. The real wage hasn't increased even though today's 30 year old is 51% more likely to have a college degree than his Boomer counterpart was in 1984. Millennials who didn't finish college are doing much worse, but for the most part, they're not working in insurance since it takes a college degree to get into most insurance carriers now a days. This is even more absurd since the economy is 70% more productive than it was in 1984!

We're not saying that Boomers are responsible for the damaged economic state of young workers today, or that it's their responsibility to fix it. We just want them to understand why a Millennial today might jump ship for what looks like a small salary difference at another company (or industry). Millennials are justifiably frustrated with a corporate world that downsized their parents and were mired in ethical scandals for most of their formative years. They're also justifiably annoyed at seeing how their education was so much more expensive while their income hasn't grown compared to their predecessors.

Chapter 3: What Millennials Look for at Work

"Insurers must focus on appealing to the next generation by promoting the perks and benefits they desire, including flexible work, mentoring opportunities, and corporate citizenship. Only then can they successfully combat the growing skills gap within the industry."

-2016 *Insurance Talent Trends by the Jacobson Group*

So, what the heck are those crazy kids looking for at work? This is where the book starts getting more fun, and where we can finally give you some good news!

Here's a chart of what surveys find Millennials look for at work, and how the insurance industry measures up[26]:

Millennials Want:	Does Insurance Offer It?
Challenging Work	Yes!
Making a Positive Impact in the World	Yes!
Room to Grow Their Career	Yes!

---

[26] Generational Talent Management for Insurers - Deloitte

Flexible Schedule	Somewhat
Working with the	
Latest Technology	For the most part no

Talk to anyone who has been in insurance for a long time and they'll tell you there are tons of challenging positions in the industry. Ask any claims professional, and you'll see that we absolutely make a positive impact in the world, regardless of how the media portrays us. Carly had a fellow CPCU tell her the following piece of advice which she now repeats often, "Go talk to your company's claims people. If you don't find one that has cried after paying a claim, you're in the wrong company." Insurance is an absolute necessity for the economy to function, for people to be able to take risks, and for people to get back on their feet if they do suffer a loss.

Look at your own career. If you're reading this book, chances are you are now in a managerial role and have seen significant growth in your insurance career. You are living proof that there's a lot of room to grow in insurance!

The last two are a bit harder. A flexible schedule is harder to get. An employee will likely have to prove themselves to the company first. But we do know many insurance professionals who have flexible schedules, and overall work life balance in the industry is excellent. And, we all know that the legacy systems at most companies do not qualify as "the Latest Technology." However, in recent years, the industry has recognized the need to adapt and improve the tools we use to do our work; Millennials could look on this as an opportunity to drive change in their organization if they are given the chance to give feedback and build better systems.

Millennials also look for long-term career development, a variety of experiences, a sense of purpose and meaning in their work, open social networks, and work life balance[27]. McKinsey & Company surveyed alumni of Risk Management and Insurance college programs (RMI) and found that 83% agree that the insurance industry offers good work-life balance. Ninety-three percent believe that the industry provides frequent intellectual challenges. Another 93% believe that the industry is interesting, and 94% agree that the industry provides value to society[28].

In conclusion, we already have the characteristics of an industry that Millennials want to work in, they just don't know it yet! Remember only 4% of Millennials surveyed said that they wanted to work in insurance. So what gives? Well, we just haven't been very good at selling the industry as an employer of choice, and we simply have to get better at it. Don't just take it from us. *Talent Magnet* put it this way, "There is cause for optimism. The

---

[27] Generational Talent Management for Insurers - Deloitte 2013
[28] McKinsey & Company - Building a Talent Magnet

industry's risk management jobs offer many of the qualities - including stability and social relevance - sought by young Americans."

Interestingly, even though Millennials have a bad reputation of not sticking around, Deloitte found that they're more loyal to their employers than Gen Xers, but that in return, they demand variety and continuing learning opportunities. Basically, your Millennials will stay if you can show them that you care by giving the opportunity to move around to different areas of the company and continually pushing them to learn and develop professionally. [29].

Above and beyond almost anything else, Millennials need to feel that they're making a contribution and that their work is having an effect. They want to change the world! They want to make a contribution from day one. They know they won't be around for ten years, so they're not willing to wait for five to start making a difference. Millennials also feel that anyone who's been at the exact same position for more than two years is becoming part of the furniture and not growing, so organizations need to get better at allowing them to move around more often, or they will burn out[30]. The advantage of this is that it will lead to more well rounded professionals.

---

[29] Generational Talent Management for Insurers - Deloitte 2013
[30] There Are No Jobs Millennials Won't Leave

According to a survey by Bentley University, once you're past the hygiene factors, they also really value flexible work hours (96%), great healthcare benefits (96%), frequent salary increases (94%), a fun and social office environment (86%), rapid promotions (82%), and the ability to work from home (78%)[31]. Insurance magazine PC360.com recently reported that 76% of Millennials said they are driven by more than money, and 73% say they need to see what the company is about before joining[32]. In other words, what they are looking for is meaning in their work!

The flexible work hours and the ability to work from home don't have to start right away, but they should be used from the moment a job offer is made in order to motivate them to achieve certain basic goals, such as completing training. Frequent salary increases and rapid promotions don't have to be expensive, they're simply forms of feedback and helping them feel appreciated and like they're truly accomplishing something. We'll talk more about that in Chapter 21.

---

[31] Bentley University - The Millennial Mind Goes to Work
[32] What it takes to attract and keep insurance & financial service employees - PC360

Chapter 4: Exciting Industry Efforts

"I would suggest changing the paradigm of insurance to Risk Management and to work with the Universities to create more Risk Management Programs. "
-Sharon Emek, President & CEO of Work at Home Vintage Experts[33]

Talent Magnet called for the industry to work together: "Coordinated actions are required. [...] The industry's main participants - insurers, reinsurers, brokers and agents, professional associations, and schools - must act with a unified voice to improve the industry's reputation, build awareness of the industry's opportunities among students and their advisors, expand the number of graduates from schools of insurance and risk management, and improve the education and training that risk professionals receive." We are very happy to see that the industry did listen, and some efforts are already underway to help us become more attractive to future employees! In this chapter, we give a quick overview of these efforts:

InVEST

InVEST's mission is to improve insurance literacy to students and attract new talent to the insurance industry. It's a school-to-work

---

[33] http://www.insurancejournal.com/news/national/2015/05/01/366633.htm

program that teams up with high school and college educators to provide an insurance curriculum for the students.

Professionals can volunteer to become an InVEST liaison and help students job shadow in their company, help them find internships in the industry, and hopefully, help them fall in love, so they'll want to pursue an insurance career in the future.

InVEST provides all needed materials, and the curriculum is created specifically to engage younger Millennials. And it's totally free! Believe it or not, it has existed since 1970 when the Independent Insurance Agents of Los Angeles started the program. By 2017, InVEST was active in more than 800 high schools and colleges!

Their website has some great basic information on insurance available to anyone. Our favorite part of it is the personality test to help you figure out what area of insurance you'd be a good match for! Maybe it'd be a good idea to make all your job applicants take it to help them find a good personality match!

The website looks a little dated, but the information is top notch. They also feature a map of RMI programs around the country and much more information. InVEST provides a lot of money in scholarships, a summer college program, and just a lot of generally useful information.

You can find more information at http://inVESTprogram.org.

InsureMyPath

InsureMyPath is dedicated to educating students and young professionals about the insurance industry, and especially careers in the industry. It's a collaborative insurance industry effort led by the The Institutes, The Griffith Insurance Education Foundation. It was launched in 2013.

They have a modern and attractive design, have a great explanation of what insurance is, and they make a good case as to why people should consider insurance careers. Our favorite features are the "Find Your Path" quiz and their "Real People, Real Stories" section.

More information is available at https://www.insuremypath.org/.

Insurance Careers Month

Insurance Careers Month is a grassroots collaboration "with no fundraising involved" that brings together a number of industry organizations in order to inspire young people to choose insurance as a career and share what makes the insurance industry an amazing place to work.

They have a big list of sponsors and list nine insurance CEOs as supporters. They use the Twitter hashtag #CareersTrifecta throughout the month of February and create a lot of positive buzz for the industry. Carly, Tony, and InsNerds.com are active participants!

More about them at http://insurancecareerstrifecta.org/.

BeAnActuary.com

Be An Actuary does a great job of painting the picture of what actuaries do and why an actuarial career can be very rewarding. They combine a bunch of cool features like video, a Twitter feed, and my favorite, their "How Actuaries See The World" section that really illustrates how actuaries have deep, if somewhat behind the scenes, effects on society. They have a great explanation on what actuaries do, who they work for, and even how an actuarial career can involve travelling the world. They have a detailed guide to who might be happy as an actuary, what to do in high school, and what to do in college to advance potential career chances. Good job to the Society of Actuaries and the Casualty Actuarial Society (yes, they are different organizations) for this website.

InsuringOhioFutures.com

The state of Ohio is a leader in encouraging insurance careers, and it shows. After all, they are the home base for multiple carriers, including Nationwide, State Auto, Grange, and Motorists in Columbus; Progressive in Cleveland; and Cincinnati Financial, American Modern, and Great American in Cincinnati.

The Ohio Insurance Institute created this website to attract many sources of talent into insurance careers. It has sections for Millennials, Mid-career employees, and Veterans. It includes an "Ask a Pro" section where interested people can ask a question to a current insurance professional along with some video interviews of other insurance people. Their Insurance Career Survey helps you figure out which area of insurance might be a good match for you.

InsNerds.com

InsNerds is our baby and what directly led to this book's existence. It is a completely independent insurance industry blog. InsNerds started as a place where we could write articles sharing insurance industry specific career advice that wasn't easy to find when we started in the industry. Over time, it's grown to be a lot more!

Our mission is to help young insurance professionals grow their careers, to encourage kids to pursue Risk Management & Insurance (RMI) majors in college, followed by insurance careers. We aim to help insurance companies better understand how to recruit, engage, and retain Millennial employees and to help the insurance industry look forward into the future and assess how technology might affect insurance. We are also tireless and passionate supporters of CPCU and other insurance technical designations.

We launched InsNerds in 2014, and it is completely independent and self-funded on a shoestring budget of our own personal savings. Someday we might accept sponsors, but the main career content will always remain free to the readers. Tell all your coworkers about InsNerds and feel free to share our articles with anyone who might benefit from them!

Some of our features include:

The World's Simplest Insurance Glossary: An ever growing collection of insurance terminology built using only the 1,000 most common words in the English language so it can be easily understood by a six year old child, or by anyone with only a basic comprehension of the language.

The InsNerds Bookshelf: Since "all leaders are readers," we are also both big readers and have built the Bookshelf to help other young insurance nerds find great books to read and grow with. It includes a sizeable section on insurance books, which can sometimes be hard to find, along with general business books, and some fiction (because we like to have some fun!) Each book has a description of why we think it's an important read for an insurance professional.

Regular Articles: We usually publish between one and three articles per week, and as of early 2017, we have 130+ articles online. Our calling card is that we write from the heart and give concrete, specific advice you won't find anywhere else.

Podcasts: In early 2017, we brought in industry veteran Nicholas Lamparelli as a third partner. Nick became our Chief Evangelist and Executive Producer of Profiles in Risk, the only recurring podcast about insurance careers, InsureTech startups, and insurance news. It comes out every Monday and will make your commute so much more fun!

Check it all out at https://InsNerds.com.

Efforts Abroad

DiscoverRisk.co.uk: This British effort is a lot of fun. Their colorful website is unique and it starts with an "About You" section which does a great job of making it all about the reader and how they'd love a career in insurance. They have a fun graphical personality test where people figure out what type of roles might be a good match for them and why. This is one of the most fun efforts we've seen. They even explain (in fun ways) about the CII (the British equivalent to CPCU), how risk is an international business, the history of insurance, and much more. They also have an app!

CareersInInsurance.com.au: They explain the why, what, how, and when of careers in insurance using an extensive and visually attractive website. There is a ton of content here including a board to send your resume in once they've convinced you to try it out.

What we can learn from the CPAs

The accounting industry had a similar problem to the one we face today - it was perceived as boring and simply uncool. Then the Enron collapse happened in 2001, largely because of "creative" accounting, and all of a sudden accounting started getting a lot of attention in the media. The accountants used all of this attention in a positive way and launched a big effort to convince kids that accounting is cool and a great career.

The AICPA launched Start Here Go Places[34] which was designed to appeal to 12 to 20 year olds. It was a *huge* success with millions of visitors in its first year, and after six years, it had grown to half a million registered users.

By the 2006-2007 school year, a mere five years later, 64,000 students were graduating with either a bachelor's or a masters in accounting. That was the largest number of graduates in the 36 years the AICPA had been keeping track, and it was 19% more than the survey just a couple of years before in 2003-2004[35].

The CPA's efforts resulted in a 30% increase in the number of accounting majors within five years[36] and CPA firms were able to increase their hiring by 83%[37].

Teachers in the United Kingdom

Teachers in the UK also had amazing success with a recruiting program aimed at making teaching cool to students. They started a recruiting campaign and within four years teaching climbed from being the 92nd most desirable job to first place! In the fourth year, the incoming class of teachers had the highest academic qualifications in the history of the profession. Before the

---

[34] http://StartHereGoPlaces.com
[35] http://www.seattletimes.com/business/forget-stereotypes-accounting-is-cool/
[36] McKinsey & Company - Building a Talent Magnet
[37] 2008 Trends in the Study of Accounting Graduates

campaign, their numbers had been declining by 2% per year. After the campaign, they increased by 9% per year while applications to become a teacher increased by 35% over three years[38].

[38] McKinsey & Company - Build a Talent Magnet

Chapter 5: The First Day is Crucial

According to research by the Center for Generational Kinetics for Millennials, the first day at work is of paramount importance. It's when a new employee is looking for confirmation that they made the right choice to work at a company, and it either confirms their belief that they're going to be successful, or it shatters their dreams.

If you get the first day right, they'll be texting their friends to apply for a job there. If you don't get it right, they'll be applying for other jobs by lunch, and if you really screw it up they might never come back from lunch! It's called the bathroom trip to nowhere...

Together, Carly and Tony have had seven first days at different insurance carriers and have talked to hundreds of other young insurance professionals about their first days. On average the first day in our industry looks something like this:

You show up with a big class of people starting the same day. An HR representative greets everyone, checks your legal documents, perhaps plays a marketing video about the company, and, of course, you receive some training about not harassing people. Then, if you're lucky, you get handed over to orientation. If you're not this lucky, you just get passed over to your new department which might or might not have a good 'new employee program.' Usually, your computer won't be ready for a few days, and if you're in an entry level role with no in-person customer contacts, you might never get business cards. After all, it is an unnecessary cost!

The general feel of our first day was very much that of "you need this job more than we need you, and you should be thankful we took you in." Not exactly something to get us tweeting excitedly about falling in love with the industry!

Now, allow us to draw you a vivid image of what an unforgettable first day in insurance could look like:

You show up and your new manager meets you at the door. All of the HR paperwork was already done online last week, so no time needs to be wasted on legal documents. You've also had the employee manual for a week and are already familiar with it. Your boss introduces you to your peer mentor (some companies call him your buddy or trainer). He's an employee on your team who has been with the company for a year or two and is close to your age. He's going to be your 'guide' for your first few days.

Your buddy gives you a personal tour of the facilities while getting to know you and candidly tells you some of his favorite things about working here. The gym is awesome, the cafeteria is ok, and the people are super nice. Management truly keeps an open door policy, and he feels very much at home. He is excited for his career here!

Your buddy walks you back to your manager who introduces you to the team you'll be working with. She takes you to your new work area, and your computer is ready to go... and all of the software you need is installed and working. For lunch, the entire team takes you out to a nearby restaurant, and the meeting is enjoyable. People seem to enjoy working here and with your new team.

Sometime during the afternoon, your boss takes you upstairs to meet one of the company's executives. You get a couple of minutes to chat with him or her, and they shake your hand, tell you how excited they are that you came to work for them, and that they're confident you're going to have a great career here. Their door is always open!

At the end of the day, your boss tells you what time you need to be in the next day and congratulates you again for your great decision of coming to work for this company. Before you head out, they hand you a small box with your new company business cards. They even spelled your name correctly. "Tony, this means that you are now part of XYZ Company. You now represent XYZ Company with everything you do and we are here for you. We want you to feel at home and happy here, and we look forward to you having a great career with us."

The business cards are a big deal! In many entry level insurance roles, people don't get business cards if they're not going to be meeting customers in person. Business cards cost roughly $17 for 500 cards. This is NOT the place to cut expenses. The lack of a business card tells the new employee that this is just a job, and that's the wrong message. New business cards show a new employee that they spent seven years in college and borrowed $70,000 to get a career, not just a job. Even if they never hand more than one card out, your investment was well worth it, and they will for sure hand out at least one card, even if it's just to their mother, who might be the one picking them up at the end of the day.

If you redesign their first day well, you will make it much easier for Millennials to start with the right foot forward. After you get the first day right, it's time to work on getting orientation right.

Chapter 6: Getting Orientation Right

Orientation is our only chance to get a new employee properly introduced to the industry and the company, and to get them to understand what we do. It's even more important in the insurance industry than in others since 85-90% of new entry level hires don't come from a Risk Management and Insurance (RMI) program. It's very likely that they have very little knowledge of what insurance is, how it works, or why it's important. This is the company's chance to win them over - you have to get it right!

We have found no insurance specific data, but in the overall economy only 12% of employees strongly agree that their organization does a great job of onboarding new employees[39]. Based on our own experiences and conversations with many other young insurance professionals, we would guess this number to be even lower in our industry.

Tony had two very different orientation experiences early in his insurance career that really illustrate how orientation can make or break a new employee. The first one, which was very good and set a good tone for the rest of his career, was at Farm Bureau Financial Services (FBFS) in Des Moines, Iowa. To protect the guilty, we won't mention the name of the company that put him through a less than great orientation later on.

---

[39] Gallagher's State of the American Workforce

When Tony showed up at Farm Bureau, they got a lot of things right, even during the interview. The two interviewers made it very clear that this entry level role was in a call center environment. They didn't sugar coat it. They also made it very clear that their goal was for every new call center person to spend two to three years in the call center (at most) and then grow within the company.

Every Tuesday for their first eight weeks, from twelve noon to four pm, every new employee from every part of the company would meet in the training area for orientation. They were taught the history of insurance and the history of Farm Bureau. They were taught the importance of insurance for the economy and how Farm Bureau is different from other insurance companies. They did a deep dive into how insurance works and Farm Bureau's package policy. They also spent a lot of time talking about the company culture, how friendliness is considered a key part of life at the company, and how retirees have lifetime access to the campus and workout facilities. Farm Bureau even introduced several ways to grow a career and take advantage of everything the company had to offer. Special emphasis was put on insurance designations and how to make the most out of the tuition reimbursement program and the in-house testing center.

By the end of orientation Tony felt like part of the family and had started to discover that insurance can really be a cool industry. Who would've known?!

In contrast, orientation at another major carrier was, shall we say, less engaging. Tony showed up, signed HR paperwork, watched a video about the benefits, and was unceremoniously handed over to his department. They in turn handed him and the other new hire to a trainer, put them in a classroom, and for two weeks the trainer talked extensively about the antiquated claims system they would be working on.

That's it. There was no real company-wide orientation to speak of. No introduction to the industry or how the company is different from other insurance companies. No tour of the many awesome things the company does in the community or what it stands for, and if you knew who this company was, you would be even more disappointed because they truly do contribute greatly to the communities they are in. But no. . . nothing. No education on what is insurance, how it works, or why it's important for the economy. No help figuring out how to grow in the company and/or the industry. They basically left new employees to figure everything out on their own.

Tony was very lucky Farm Bureau did such a good job, not only getting him excited about the industry but also putting him on the right path to grow. That good advice is the reason he was able to grow and is still in the industry. His time at Farm Bureau very much planted the seeds that led him to fall in love with the industry, eventually start InsNerds, and write this book. That's the magic of a good orientation program!

We're not saying Farm Bureau's orientation was perfect, but it's certainly in the right direction of what we should be doing all over the industry. To really hit it out of the park, we recommend adding an exploration of the different areas of the company and what they do, a presentation by claims people, and even videos of real customers talking about how the company helped them get back on their feet after a disaster. Perhaps add an explicit discussion on what different careers paths at the company might look like. Also make sure you spend some time discussing the demographic crisis, the very low unemployment in the industry, and how growing in insurance is completely doable and not really that hard for those willing to put the work forth and do the right things.

Finally, ultra brownie points if you fly all new hires to headquarters for a two to three day orientation focused on making them feel like part of the family, getting them to really understand the company culture, and giving them the tools to grow. Yes, it's expensive at probably $2,500 to $5,000 per employee, but the loyalty and buy-in you get is worth it, and overall, it's much cheaper than the $25,000 or more that it would likely cost to replace them. Remember that many companies spend as much as $100,000 to replace a first year employee[40].

---

[40] Solving the Insurance Industry Talent Crisis by Investing in RMI Graduates - IRMI Sept 2015

Chapter 7: Give Constant and Honest Feedback

Millennials grew up getting constant feedback from their parents, school counselors, coaches, and everybody else who helped raise them. They also grew up playing video games. Recent research by Dr. Jane McGonigal of UC Berkeley has found that one of the reasons video games can be so addicting is because they give constant feedback.

There is a very popular misconception that Millennials require constant *positive* feedback, but that's not true. They're absolutely comfortable with getting constructive feedback, but worry much more if they get no feedback, which is what is truly demotivating for a Millennial.

The traditional corporate system of managers keeping notes on an employee's performance and not sharing it with them until their yearly review simply doesn't work for Millennials.

Research has found that Millennials find Annual Reviews to be a big turn off. Only 15% prefer formal Quarterly Reviews and only 1% like Annual Reviews[41]. What they want is ongoing feedback. They're used to texting, tweeting, Skype, Instagram, SnapChat, and instant messaging. All of their communication channels are

---

[41] Millennial Mindset Understanding Millennials

real-time. Millennials are so used to constant communication and feedback that annual reviews simply no longer work[42].

If they're doing a great job but not receiving feedback, they'll start to worry things aren't going well, become disengaged, and probably start looking for the next job. After all, they have no idea if they're about to get fired! For a Millennial, no news is bad news! Only 23% of all employees agree that their managers provide them with meaningful feedback[43].

On the other hand, if they're doing something wrong, nothing will alienate a Millennial employee more than being told during their Annual Review that they've been doing something wrong for months and hadn't been told. Don't save things up for the review! By the time a Millennial shows up at the Annual Review, it should be a formality, and there should be no surprises. Besides, it's a win/win to share constructive feedback quickly. Why wait until later to correct bad behaviors?

Feedback needs to be constant, and constant in this case means weekly. We know that sounds like a ton of work, and you're thinking, "If I have to give every one of my people weekly feedback, I won't have time to get anything else done. Why don't you just take me out back and get rid of me right now?" We feel

---

[42] How Millennials Want to Work and Live - Gallup
[43] State of the American Workforce - Gallup

your pain, but don't panic about it. Here's the key thing to remember: Feedback should be weekly, but it doesn't need to be anything formal. It doesn't need to take half an hour. It can be something as simple as stopping by your Millennial's desk for five minutes and quickly and candidly sharing what they're doing well, what they need to improve, and asking them if they need any help or have questions. Also, it has to be specific, no platitudes. That's it. Done. It takes just five minutes.

That being said, even weekly might not be enough. As crazy as it might sound, a global survey of Millennials by Universum found that 25% of Millennials said they expect feedback every day, if not instantly[44]! Let that sink in for a moment.

Here's what it might sound like, "Hi Tony. You have a minute to chat? I just wanted to let you know I'm hearing good things from your agents, they love working with you, and you're doing a great job for them. Mike Simpson at Jones' Brokerage was especially thankful that you were able to turn that quote around in a rush. However, I need you to keep a closer eye on renewals. New business is still crucial, but we lost a big renewal last month and you didn't know the account was being marketed until after we had lost it. Let me know if you need help on best practices for

---

[44] http://theirf.org/am-site/themes/IRF/download.php?file=http%3A%2F%2Ftheirf.org%2Fam-site%2Fmedia%2Fgenerations-in-the-workforce-marketplacepreferences-in-rewards-recognition-incentives.pdf page 29

renewals. What's going on on your side? Do you need any help? Do you have any questions? Everything going well?"

Basically, Millennials don't want bosses, they want coaches. They want managers who coach them to grow and improve. They also need their managers to value them as people, not just as employees[45]. This will be a hard transition for old-style command and control managers, and those who get used to it and get good at it will unlock immense passion and performance from their Millennials.

If you're not very comfortable giving feedback, or if you'd like to learn one of the best simple techniques to give feedback, listen to the 'Giving Effective Feedback" episode of Manager Tools which can be found at https://www.manager-tools.com/2005/07/giving-effective-feedback.

One word of warning though, some Millennials have never received real constructive feedback and might be shocked the first few times they're told they're not quite perfect. When Tony founded the Sacramento Chapter of Nationwide's Gen Y Associate Resource Group, he gave the first version of his Retaining and Engaging Millennials in the Insurance Industry presentation to the local management group. During that session, he recommended constant and honest feedback.

---

[45] How Millennials Want to Work and Live - Gallup

A female director took his advice and gave a female employee some tough constructive feedback, and the employee broke down and started crying right in front of the director. The director, who had spent 20 years breaking glass ceilings in a male dominated industry, was appalled, and she let Tony know her unhappiness with what happened.

After that, we started recommending the book *Thanks for the Feedback* by Douglas Stone and Sheila Heen. This book teaches managers how to properly give feedback, and most importantly, it teaches Millennials that feedback is a gift to be cherished, accepted, analyzed, and acted upon. We highly recommend giving it to all your employees before deploying the constant feedback Millennials need. If it were up to us, this book would be mandatory reading in college, and we would hand it out in orientation to every new employee.

Tony himself got some very tough, constructive feedback while going through a finance leadership development program. His manager made it clear that while Tony is a passionate and knowledgeable insurance professional, he's just not a finance person. She didn't pull any punches. It hurt, a lot, but he was very thankful, and as he looks back years later, he's even more thankful for the candid feedback. That conversation probably saved him years of wasting his time in a position that he just wasn't well suited for, and today, he's much happier in the sales management and underwriting type roles he's been working in since. Constructive feedback is crucial, and it changes careers (and companies) for the better!

The research is very clear, when it comes to Millennials, managers who provide constant and consistent communication and feedback have more engaged and productive employees. In fact, managers providing frequent feedback report that 44% of Millennial employees respond positively to engagement surveys versus only 20% of those who work under managers who don't provide frequent feedback[46].

---

[46] How Millennials Want to Work and Live - Gallup

Chapter 8: A Clear and Objective Performance Evaluation System

"Employees largely do not believe that current performance discussions provide clarity or feel meaningful. They do not believe they have a voice in the conversation or a legitimate shot at meeting their goals."

-Gallup's State of the American Workplace

Sadly, in our overly litigious country, the corporate performance evaluation system is used mostly to protect the company from wrongful termination lawsuits. Managers are required to have well documented conversations with employees about their performance, so if a termination has to happen, the company can defend itself. This is a sad waste of the performance evaluation system. Only 21% of employees strongly agree that their performance is managed in a way that motivates them, and only 18% believe that employees who perform better grow faster at their organization[47]. Even executives agree; 58% believe that the current performance management approach doesn't encourage employee engagement or higher performance[48].

The evaluation system must evolve to be much more. It should be outcome-driven, and it should be what keeps Millennials focused

---

[47] Gallup - State of the American Workforce
[48] Harvard Business Review April 2015 - Reinventing Performance Management

and on task. They need to know that what they are working on will be evaluated often, candidly, fairly, and in an objective manner. Most importantly, they need to know ahead of time how the game is being scored.

Annual Performance Reviews have become so destructive that companies such as Deloitte, Adobe, Accenture, and GE are getting rid of them entirely[49]! An incredible amount of manager and HR time gets wasted on them, while the return on that investment is questionable at best, and in most companies, probably negative. Their effect on morale is destructive, and quite honestly, nobody benefits from them.

Whether they call them "check-ins" (Adobe), "design calls" (Deloitte), or "touchpoints" (GE), they are all transitioning towards more frequent and more informal one-on-ones. We are big fans of one-on-ones and encourage you to read up on them. Our favorite source for information about how to properly do one-on-ones is Manager Tools (http://www.manager-tools.com), which includes them as part of their Management Trinity.

The companies that are leading the way have reported great results. Deloitte said, "The feedback we're getting already from our employees is that they are ecstatic around this process." GE got a "fivefold productivity increase" within 12 months. Adobe

---

[49] https://getlighthouse.com/blog/get-rid-of-the-performance-review/

saved "80,000 hours of manager's time in the annual review process; and saw a 30% reduction in voluntary turnover."[50]

Y Size recommends doing structured performance reviews once a month. Yeah, we know it takes you a long time to prepare for the company mandated yearly performance reviews, but those are just a formality. What we're recommending is less formal, and much more important in keeping Millennials engaged.

Many companies make the mistake of measuring too many things. If you're holding them accountable to more than seven measurements, they're going to feel out of control and disengaged.

Be very clear from the beginning: How will this job be measured? What does success look like? What do they need to do to grow to the next level? Which numbers are important and where exactly do they need to be for an acceptable, good, or very good performance?

Millennials grew up in an era of grade inflation and where all participants got a ribbon (sometimes a trophy). Many are getting to their first professional jobs without having had a bad grade in their lives. The typical corporate evaluation system on a scale of five, where 80% of employees get a three, is very disengaging. If

---

[50] https://getlighthouse.com/blog/get-rid-of-the-performance-review/

this is the system you have to work under, then you need to get ahead of the problem. From the very beginning, when you give them their goals, explain that a three means they did everything that was expected of them and they are doing fine. Make it abundantly clear if there's a limit on the number of fours and fives that can be given.

Something like, "Hey Ariel, you're sharp so I bet you kept straight A's in high school and college. Sometimes, with people who have always been great students, they get disappointed once they hit the corporate world because of our evaluation system. At the end of the year, we'll sit back down and go over how you did on the goals I gave you, and you'll get a number score on a scale from one to five. It's not a grading scale like what you used in school. Most people get a three, and it means you're doing your job well, doing everything we want you to be doing, and that you're developing according to plan. We give out very few fours and almost no fives. Fours are reserved for those who truly went above and beyond the call of duty, and fives are essentially for people who had giant impacts on the overall company."

Having this kind of candid conversation up front will save you a lot of trouble by keeping Millennials from feeling like they failed when actually they did a fine job. It really helps in the transition from collegiate to corporate environments!

Mary started a new position at her company in a brand new department. She accepted a salary she was happy with and because the job involved some selling she was also offered a $25,000 bonus target. This was the highest bonus she had ever had the chance of getting, and she was pumped for it. Because this was a new department, they did not give her a specific goal that she was supposed to hit. They hadn't yet created the actual formula to determine how much of the large bonus she would get at the end of the year. She worked hard, helped improve processes, helped trained a new team member, and even took on some projects well outside of her normal job duties. Overall, she loved it, and at the end of the year, her boss called her to let he know she would be getting $23,000 in bonus money. She had never gotten a bonus that large and was happy about that, but she couldn't help to be disturbed by not knowing how the bonus was calculated and by not knowing the goals ahead of time.

Millennials grew up with structured lives participating in extracurricular activities, and parents who scheduled playdates for them. In school, the syllabus always told them from the very beginning of the semester how they would be graded and exactly what they had to do to be successful. They find it very frustrating when they're not given all of the pertinent information up front on how they will be measured. They want to do a killer job for you! Give them the chance to do that by being transparent with the evaluation system and the goals that are important for their current job. Also help them paint the picture of where in the company they might be a good fit next, and what they need to do to get there. In exchange, you will have much more engaged Millennials!

Gallup reports that there is nothing more disengaging to a Millennial than a performance evaluation system based on subjective factors. You must evaluate them on objective performance measures. "Millennials are very practical and results-oriented. They don't want any subjectivity at work. They want to be told clearly what's expected of them and the best way to do the job. They also want to know that they'll be evaluated fairly.[51]"

The most comprehensive research on performance rating was done by Michael Mount, Steven Scullen, and Maynard Goff and published in the *Journal of Applied Psychology in 2000*. It found that 62% of the variance in ratings was due to individual raters' subjective perceptions, and actual performance counted for only 21%[52]. The researchers concluded, "Although it is implicitly assumed that the ratings measure the performance of the ratee, most of what is being measured by the ratings is the unique rating tendencies of the rater. Thus ratings reveal more about the rater than they do about the ratee."[53]

---

[51] There's No Job Millennials Won't Leave - Gallup
[52] Understanding the Latent Structure of Job Performance Ratings - American Psychological Association
[53] How People Evaluate Others in Organizations, book edited by Michael London

Millennials are a generation that will question everything, and they have a hard time following instructions unless they understand the "why" behind it. So, make the reasoning explicit. They have very little tolerance for things that don't make sense and haven't been explained to them. For example, they will totally understand that they have to dress up on a day a client is visiting, but if their day-to-day job involves no in-person time with clients, many of them will be questioning your business casual dress code. After all, if jeans are acceptable on Friday, why not for the other days? Unless you can put together a solid explanation of this, they'll have a hard time buying it.

McKinsey reports that what high-performing companies do differently than everyone else is building a best-in-class performance management system. Evaluations are consistent throughout the company, and everyone is measured objectively. Measuring individual performance in this way makes it easy to differentiate rewards and really engage your top performers through better pay, bonuses, recognition, and extra time off. Also, they're swift in dealing with low performers[54].

Ultimately, what we need is a better, more humane, less subjective, and more motivating performance evaluation system. Helping you build that is well beyond the scope of this book, but

---

[54] McKinsey and Company - Talent Magnet

we recommend you start with the *Reinventing Performance Management* article in the April 2015 issue of Harvard Business Review.

Chapter 9: Ask for Their Opinions

When Tony was ten years old, his divorced mom was in the process of buying her first home as a single woman. She involved Tony from the beginning, and he had a large say in where they ended up living. This is not an uncommon experience for a Millennial. Then, we went to college, and schools continued the trend by asking him at the end of each semester what he thought of each of his professors. Most Millennials grew up being asked frequently for their opinion, and they are used to that style. When they arrive in the corporate world, they're sorely disappointed to find that no one asks for their opinions.

We completely understand that they're inexperienced, and you won't be able to implement most of their opinions, but the simple act of being asked makes Millennials feel listened to and makes it it easier to become engaged in the company. It's a free way of increasing commitment and employee happiness.

It's not just Millennials that like to be asked for their opinion. There's research indicating that older adults living in assisted living facilities live longer, healthier lives if they have control over some aspects of their living situation, even if it's minor things like the type of plants they have in their room, or whether they would like jello or pudding for dessert.

Julia, a Millennial, worked for a manager that never asked for her team's opinion on anything. The manager was sure she knew how to do it better than they did, that's why she made the big bucks! She tapped Julia to supervise the team, and the first thing she did was set up one-on-ones with everyone and asked them for their opinion. A couple of the team members suggested that a particular billing process could easily be changed and improved. Julia took their advice and changed the process. The ironic thing is that the boss loved the change and loudly exclaimed that he wished people had shared their opinion on it long before. Also, turnover in the team decreased while Julia was supervising the team!

Chapter 10: Become a Mentor

Mentoring is extremely important. It facilitates knowledge transfer between the generations, helps build a cohesive culture, and fits very well with Millennials who grew up being mentored by parents, teachers, and coaches.

A few years back, we started noticing many of our Millennial peers burning out from their insurance jobs and started researching the problem. We compared our industry to other industries that Millennials reportedly love, and our first thought was that it was a matter of money. How can Facebook and Google get Millennials to bleed and pull all-nighters for the company while we can't seem to get them to stay for five years?

While we first thought it was purely a monetary issue, we soon came to a second thought that it was about the 'cool' factor of being able to say you work for a brand your peers love. But after much research, and many conversations with friends who work for the tech companies in San Francisco and elsewhere, we have come to the conclusion that it's not a matter of money *or* brand. The one thing that almost all of the companies that consistently show up as the places where Millennials are dying to work at have in common is they all have formal mentoring programs. Some pay a lot (Google), and some pay very little (Teach for America), but they have all figured out the mentoring piece. They also have figured out how to get Millennials to believe in their mission, and mentoring helps immensely with that.

Mentoring not only buys loyalty to the company and makes it much easier for a Millennial to figure out what is valued at their company and how to grow, it also gets them trained and productive at a much faster rate. After all, if you might only have them for 11 months, you need them to make a difference right away! Mentoring also helps teach Millennials how to successfully navigate the company and the industry, giving them a sounding board and helping them feel connected, which is something they absolutely expect.

It's particularly important today because of many Millennials very limited work experience prior to graduating from college. It is one of the ways to create a bridge between the generations and build understanding. Remember, many Millennials simply haven't had the right advice and might turn into great employees once they do. What a Boomer thought was "common sense" when they first showed up, they probably learned in an earlier job during high school or college. Many Millennials didn't have that advantage.

Once the mentoring system is built and well oiled, it's also time to consider a reverse mentoring program where your Millennials can help more mature executives understand things like technology, and maybe even work life balance!

Chapter 11: Set A Clear Career Path

Jerry used to work with us at a large insurance carrier. He came in straight out of college and took an entry level claims role, exactly the kind of role that has a high turnover rate and tends to chew people right out of the industry. After his first year, he was disappointed but trying to figure it out. He was looking for ways to grow and asking his manager for advice. His manager kept telling him he was doing "a fine job" and just needed to "keep doing what you're doing." He stumbled around different ideas on how to get promoted, worked hard to keep his numbers up, and started to get burnt out. Just before hitting his second year at the company, he left to go sell mortgages at a large national bank. When we asked him why he was leaving, his main complaint was that he didn't feel he had a future in the industry, and he felt stuck. Unfortunately, this is the most common complaint we hear from frustrated Millennials who are considering leaving insurance.

What if his manager had told Jerry at the very beginning of his career about the different paths that he could grow into and what the timeline looked like? "If you get your AIC (Associate in Claims) and keep your job performance in line, in two to three years, you can probably qualify to get off of the phones and take a more advanced claims role.

If your interest is in becoming a manager, volunteering to lead a project or taking a leadership role in a volunteer organization would be a great way to develop your skills. Also, getting your CPCU would be a great way to show you're committed to the industry, or your MBA which would show commitment to becoming a manager."

What if he had gotten educated about the industry and the career possibilities for him? Maybe, if someone had clued him in about the demographic crisis and how it's pretty much mathematically guaranteed to create amazing career opportunities for young insurance professionals who invest in themselves in the right ways, he would have stuck around. If someone had shared some excitement about the industry and about his own future career, there's a good chance he would have stayed.

Instead, he left. The company invested two years into getting him to understand how to do claims, and they didn't get their investment back. It's not shame on him, it's shame on the company! They failed him. They assumed that since they were able to figure it out on their own that he would be able to do that too.

Millennials grew up in an age of instant gratification, and they were constantly told by every important adult in their life that they were special and would do amazing things in life. What they may not have heard is that it takes hard work to get there, and that success is not a straight line. In order to really engage them, companies need to balance out those lessons with new ones to help them grow.

When an entry level employee joins the company, they should learn about the different career paths available and the things that they can do to increase their chances of pursuing one of those career paths. This process should start as early as the offer letter and should be reinforced through orientation, job shadow opportunities during the first few years of employment, and in every performance conversation with their manager.

Painting this explicit image of the different career paths that may be pursued might feel like you're spoonfeeding them, but it's absolutely necessary in order to keep them. Put yourself in their shoes. If you had grown up in a world with no promise of lifetime employment, with depressed salaries compared to your education, and with large student loans for that education, would you be staying at a company or an industry that doesn't give you a solid preview of how you can grow?

Another way seasoned professionals can help is by updating their LinkedIn profiles, including their entire job history. When Millennials find someone in the company that they admire and they want to grow up to be in their shoes, the natural thing for them to do is to look them up on LinkedIn and try to dissect how they got to their current role. If your LinkedIn profile looks something like the following and a Millennial admirer looks you up, they won't have any idea how you got to your present position, and it will reinforce in their head the idea that they should be able to make Vice President by their second or third year in the company. That doesn't help anyone!

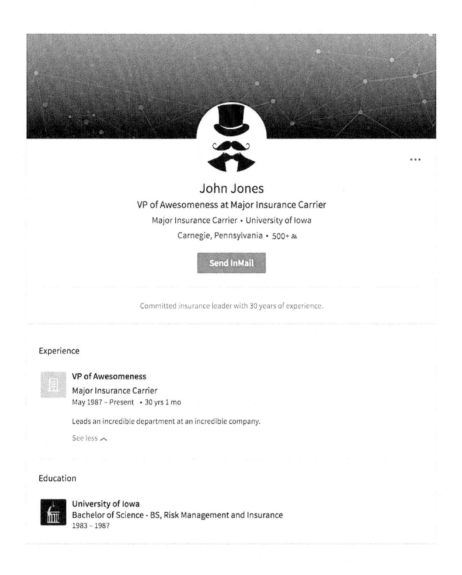

John Jones

VP of Awesomeness at Major Insurance Carrier

Major Insurance Carrier • University of Iowa

Carnegie, Pennsylvania • 500+ ஃ

Send InMail

Committed insurance leader with 30 years of experience.

Experience

VP of Awesomeness

Major Insurance Carrier

May 1987 – Present • 30 yrs 1 mo

Leads an incredible department at an incredible company.

See less ⌃

Education

University of Iowa

Bachelor of Science - BS, Risk Management and Insurance

1983 – 1987

Instead, fill out your LinkedIn profile with every job you've had, and maybe even the other awesome things that helped you get to where you are: projects, classes, designations, volunteer experiences, etc. Show them what got you where you are, and they will be much more likely to figure out how to grow in the industry!

For a great example of an amazingly well filled out LinkedIn profile check out Mark Pizzi. Mr. Pizzi is a beloved long-time Nationwide Insurance executive who has been at the company since 1978 and has his entire 39 year career at the company chronicled in his LinkedIn profile - every job since he became a Personal Lines Underwriter straight out of college! Check it out at https://www.linkedin.com/in/markpizzi/ it's truly something to see. Thank you Mark for your leadership and example!

It is also helpful for Millennials to see job descriptions with every job and special projects at every level, but honestly he's already gone above and beyond. Maybe some day we'll start sending special "InsNerds Certified Awesome LinkedIn Profile" printed certificates to insurance execs with very detailed profiles!

Just remember, if we can't see your path, we can't follow in your footsteps. Secure your legacy, shine some light on your path, and help the next generation grow a little bit easier.

To finish up this chapter, we'd like to tell you two contrasting stories.

Miranda had a few years of experience in a small insurance agency before finishing college. Once she got her fancy new degree in Political Science, she ended up unable to find a better paying job in her field and instead, reluctantly, accepted a position at a major insurance carrier.

Her entry level position was very much a call center type environment where her time was strictly measured, training opportunities were limited to learning the company's antiquated systems, and she was encouraged to sell to hurried customers on an auto dial. Time on call was the primary measure of success the department cared about, but it also measured 75+ other factors over which she felt she had very little control.

After two and a half years in the call center, she had become one of their more successful employees, based on keeping the 'Time on Call' measure down. From her perspective, at the call center, her only career path option was to become a supervisor, all of whom had grown up in the call center. She didn't particularly want that job, so she figured that there was just no future for her in this industry.

Shortly after her three year anniversary, she had become so discouraged with insurance that she decided to use her great GPA from college to go to law school instead. When she got the acceptance letter from a decent law school, she went ahead and put in her two weeks notice. Her supervisor was very surprised and tried to talk her out of leaving by telling her she was a great employee and even tried to offer her a small raise. At the end of the exit interview, she told the HR representative, "I don't know what type of law I want to practice, the one thing I know is I don't want to do anything else in insurance!"

The company and the industry both lost a smart, hard working, young professional who left not because she hated her job, or was bad at it, but because she did not see a path for a future career in the company and the industry. In her eyes, insurance will always be a call center with no future. The sad part is that we know insurance can be an amazing career once you get past those entry level jobs! She could have easily grown into Underwriting, Field Claims, or maybe even Product if she had gotten the right advice. The industry failed to tell her, and she had no easy way to figure it out.

James worked the front desk at a hospital and did basic office management and scheduling functions. He was very lucky that the hospital chain's headquarter office was located in the same city.

As soon as he started in this job, which he thought of as a temporary job, not a career, the company started telling him about all the different growth opportunities in that industry. Every conversation with his supervisor included a development discussion with specific things he could do to grow. Most importantly, every six months a manager would sit down with him to review his progress on getting prepared for the type of role he would really be passionate about.

Finally, after only 18 months and a few interviews, he got an offer as a Process Analyst at headquarters that he gladly accepted! Now he's a very happy employee and is even telling his friends to apply at the company's hospitals throughout the region. "Don't worry about finding the perfect role right away. Get your foot in the door where you can. Do a good job. The company will help you figure out where to go long-term. They're really into growing their people!"

Imagine how well this strategy would work in our call centers. All of the bright, eager, young people that we hire into our customer service centers and our claims centers could benefit from being treated like James. Our companies would benefit by getting referrals for more hardworking employees and by growing employees who feel committed to the company.

Chapter 12: Assume Good Intentions and Lack of Experience

Y Size tells the story of a Baby Boomer business owner who was hiring for an entry level role in his small company. A Millennial was scheduled to interview at 8:30 am and showed up about ten minutes late, looking disheveled, unshaven, and breathing heavily from the rush.

The business owner came out to the lobby, and once he saw the kid with this shirt tails untucked, sighed loudly and promptly sent him home. "I can already see that you're not interested in this job, let's just go ahead and call it a day. I'm sorry." The Millennial was very surprised and replied defensively, "No, I REALLY want this job. I took two busses to get here!"

The Boomer had a moment of wisdom and said, "Ok. Here's what we're going to do. Come back tomorrow at 8:30 am. I want you here ten minutes early, shaved, dressed in a proper suit and tie, wearing proper formal shoes and matching belt, with a portfolio in hand. When I come out to greet you, you will get up, shake my hand firmly, and look at me in the eyes confidently. If you do all of this, I promise I'll hire you." The Millennial agreed and went on his way, and the Boomer thought he'd never see him again. Hopefully, the rascal at least learned his lesson. Good riddance!

The next day at 8:20 am, the Millennial showed up for his interview and followed all of the great advice he had received the previous morning. The business owner was impressed and followed through on his promise to hire him. To his surprise, the kid turned out to be a solid employee!

We absolutely love this story because it illustrates in a memorable way one of the key things that people don't know about Millennials. Most people know that Millennials are the best educated generation in US history, but they don't realize that they are also coming to the workforce with much less work and life experience than previous generations!

It's natural to look at a 23 year old and think of yourself at 23. At 23 years old, chances are Boomers didn't consider themselves kids, but rather, adults. They were done with college. They were married, maybe even had their first (or second) child on the way. They owned a car and were probably working on saving up enough money for a down payment on a house. The 23 year old Millennial is likely still behaving like a kid.

Psychologists have even created a new term "adultolescent" for this phenomenon. A portmanteau of the words "adult" and "adolescent," meaning a person who is a physically mature adult but still has many of the interests of a teenager. Basically, they just haven't really grown up yet. This is a social phenomenon probably caused by increasing lifespans (so they're in no hurry to grow up) and having grown up in an affluent society that lavished too much attention on them as children.

This is not just a US phenomenon either. In Costa Rica, where Tony grew up, traditionally, kids don't move out of their parents' homes until they get married, and parents charging their adult children rent is a big social taboo. To complicate matters further, the seismically active country has no basements, making it impossible to banish them to the basement! Millennials are getting married later so they are staying at the parent's home later. . . even after graduating from college! The biggest problem many of Tony's parents' friends complain about now is having too many new cars and no place to park them, since they have two or three kids out of college with good jobs and no intention to move out!

Back to the US, Millennials followed their parents' advice and focused on extra-curriculars, not on part time work while they went to school. And they might never have had a professional job before they graduated college. Many just haven't received the right advice from their overly permissive Boomer parents and just don't know any better.

All Boomers need to do is give them that advice and then give them a chance to follow it, and they might end up with a great (and very thankful) employee!

Carly can attest to this. She worked full time through college at an insurance agent's office. The principal at the office spent a good amount of time giving her candid feedback and teaching her the mores of professional life. She is grateful to her former employer for taking the time and putting in the effort to help her become a more polished professional and quickly learn about things that are important to more experienced professionals.

Even McKinsey Consulting, which pays six figure salaries to new MBA graduates and is harder to get into than Harvard, has figured out that it makes more sense to explicitly advise Millennials on how to apply, interview, and get a job at McKinsey than to reject them without giving them a chance. They created a talent recruiting website where they instruct Millennials interested in working at McKinsey on how to dress for the interview, what to bring, and even what kind of questions they'll get and what kind of answers the interviewer is looking for. They figured out it doesn't make sense to lose out on great talent just because he or she is a little rough around the edges and hasn't yet received the right advice.

Also, there's an important concept that we could benefit from understanding: The Critical Difference Between Mistakes and Missteps.

Imagine I draw a five by five hopscotch on the floor and label it with numbers from 1 to 25:

It looks something like this:

21	22	23	24	25
16	17	18	19	20
11	12	13	14	15
6	7	8	9	10
1	2	3	4	5

Then I ask you to stand in square one and tell you that there's a secret pattern to get to square 25. If you take a step outside of that pattern I blow a whistle and penalize you. The first time you step outside the pattern I have in my head, I'm going to blow the whistle and then verbally warn you that you made a mistake. The second time, I'm going to write you up and put it in your permanent file. The third time, I'm going to have a formal meeting, and the fourth time you're fired.

That sounds pretty scary, doesn't it?

When you take a step onto a number you haven't been on before and you hear the whistle, that's a misstep. If you step on that same number you should have already known was wrong again a second time, that's a mistake.

To make the most out of our young talent we need to understand that they come from a different world than Boomers do and that they haven't had the same life experience, work experience, and advice that Boomers benefited from.

Let's mentor them and help them grow when they inevitably make missteps, and only when missteps become repeated mistakes, let's then take the time to discipline. Focus on helping them learn not only what mistake they made but also what the bigger effect on the department and the company was because of that mistake.

In his seminal book *Winning*, Jack Welch tells the story of how, in 1960, as a 24 year old new engineer at General Electric, he made a huge mistake (or should it be a misstep?) and - literally - accidentally blew up a multi-million dollar plant!

He was incredibly lucky that the explosion happened in the middle of the night, and nobody was hurt or killed. His boss sent him to New York to explain to the higher ups what had happened. Welch was entirely sure he was fired. Maybe they would even press charges. His career was clearly over!

But, that's not what happened. In his infinite wisdom, the big boss asked him what happened and what he learned from his mistake.

Then he said, "Ok, go back to work." Welch was very confused. "Aren't you going to fire me?"

"No," replied the wise man. "We just spent millions of dollars teaching you a very expensive lesson and now I know you will never make this mistake again."

Now, that is wisdom! As you know, Jack Welch grew up to become long-time CEO of GE and one of the most recognized corporate managers of the 20th Century. Nothing gains loyalty like a boss who turns our mistakes into a positive learning experience.

Chapter 13: Tell Them About CPCU and Other Insurance Education

It is no secret that Tony and Carly are CPCU fanatics. If you read InsNerds or listen to Profiles in Risk, you will likely find a mention of CPCU once every three minutes. There is a very good reason for this!

When Tony started at Farm Bureau Financial Services (FBFS) in the Express Claims Call Center, he was halfway through a three year part time Saturday MBA program at Iowa State (Go Cyclones!). During FBFS' excellent eight week orientation program, the trainer talked about insurance designations and special emphasis was put on CPCU, which he referred to as "the granddaddy of the designations, something like a master's degree in insurance."

He explained that studying for insurance designations was a great way to grow in the company and in the industry, and that the company offered a small bonus every time you passed a designation, so it was "like being paid to be a part time student." Best of all, he explained that you can take whatever designations you earned with you if you leave the company, and that other companies in the industry also value them highly.

Tony was sold! He had already created the habit of studying every day for his MBA, so it seemed like a no brainer to just add the insurance books on top. He was also intensely curious what the heck insurance education taught. How much could there possibly be to learn about insurance? Today he feels silly even typing that last sentence!

As soon as his supervisor allowed him, he got started on Intro to Insurance and then on INS 21. Farm Bureau paid for the tests up front, provided the books for free, and he could take them up to two times before having to pay for it himself. They also had an in-house testing center. When somebody passed a test, an email from the boss would go to the whole department and everybody would congratulate you.

Tony got his Associate in Claims (AIC) and Associate in General Insurance (AINS) within a few months, added them to LinkedIn, changing his name (and signature) to "Tony Cañas, AINS, AIC." Pretty quickly, he was recruited away from the call center to work in a more in-depth claims role at Nationwide Insurance, where he also completed his CPCU.

Nationwide had an army of claims, call center, and processing professionals who were all entry level and wanted to try their hand at underwriting, so underwriting was hard to get into! Every job opening for an Underwriter would get hundreds of applications that pretty much looked the same: a college degree and two years of entry level insurance experience. It's hard to get noticed in that environment!

Following the great advice he got at Farm Bureau, Tony quickly got his CPCU and within three weeks landed a job as a Farm Underwriter with Nationwide Agribusiness. Only two years into his insurance career, he had made it to exactly the role he wanted to be at. A lifelong love affair with insurance and insurance education was cemented!

Many insurance professionals take longer to start pursuing designations because they don't hear the advice that Tony got. Carly is in this group. The agency that she started at firmly believed in education and professional development, but as in many agencies, the primary opportunities for development are through continuing education or local networking groups. Since the agency principal and company staff who visited didn't recommend designations, Carly was unaware that they might be beneficial. When she moved to Des Moines and took a sales role in a call center, designations were mentioned offhandedly but never pushed. After meeting Tony at the Gen Y Associate Resource Group development meeting, he invited her to lunch. Tony explained how much he had learned by doing CPCU, and he told her that he had done it in a year. Carly's competitive streak was ignited, and she bet Tony that she could also finish in a year. She knew that she was planning to start her MBA and wouldn't want to split her attention between the two. To her great surprise, the next morning, she had an email from Tony with a plan of what she would need to study and when in order to win "the bet." He basically volunteered to be her accountability partner, and a great friendship was born.

Cute story aside, Carly also loves CPCU because of what she learned in the process, and her continued involvement in the CPCU Society. Completing the designation ought to be your employee's first step. After that, encourage them to continue using the Society's networking and professional development opportunities. Both Carly and Tony have benefited from their involvement, and they would also both tell you that it's a fantastic opportunity to give back to the industry by helping to drive the conversation and improve educational opportunities for all professionals in the industry. That's precisely the key point we're trying to make. Insurance designations aren't just fantastic for the employee's careers. They're a win/win/win!

The employee wins because they can learn and grow. The company wins because the employee becomes a much more well rounded and knowledgeable insurance professional with a solid background to grow in any area of the industry and understands the 30,000 foot view of insurance. **The industry wins because people who get their CPCUs are more valuable within the**

industry than outside of it. Contrary to an MBA, which focuses on business in general, and might lead them to leave the industry for other pastures, the CPCU is completely insurance focused and not only opens doors, but also makes it financially difficult to leave the industry since you're worth more here than elsewhere.

Your favorite nerds - Tony and Carly - have spent years as part of the CPCU Society's New Designee Committee, whose main purpose is hosting the New Designee Open House at the yearly CPCU Society Annual Meeting. The beauty of this event is that it allows them to meet hundreds of New Designees who just completed their designation each year and to connect with them, and get them motivated to keep growing their insurance careers, involvement in the CPCU Society, and pumped up to encourage others to do the same.

Out of the hundreds of mostly young insurance professionals who they've met at the Open House, they know of exactly one that left the industry. His dream was to open a restaurant and he left insurance to go do that with this wife. Funnily enough his delicious restaurant is located blocks from Tony's apartment in Atlanta and they are friends to this day. Other than him, not a single one of their CPCU friends have left the industry. For most, it has been a true career maker leading to promotions, raises, interesting projects, and an overall fulfilling career.

They key point that we need to understand is very simple: **Once they get their CPCU they will not leave the industry!** They might leave the company, but we're still ahead. If you follow all of our advice, hopefully you'll be able to keep most of your best ones!

Carly and Tony are CPCU fanatics, because that's what worked for them, but CPCU is not the only game in town. If you work in the life insurance side, CLU probably makes more sense. For those in professional liability, RPLU seems to be the big name. On the agency and broker side, CIC is the one we hear about the most. The point works for all of them because they all do the same thing - they make you more valuable in the industry than outside of it so you're likely to stay.

Tony held a wide variety of jobs at Nationwide from claims to underwriting to finance and finally sales management. Yet, he's convinced the most valuable thing he did for Nationwide was motivating 70+ people to start their CPCU. Not only was it the most valuable thing he *did*, it was the most valuable thing he *could have done*, and he did it with no budget and nothing more than enthusiasm and creative use of some of the company's collaboration tools. No reason you can't do the same at your company!

Chapter 14: Internships and Apprenticeships

It's much easier to get a young employee to work for an insurance company if we get them early with an internship or an apprenticeship, rather than trying to get them to work in insurance after graduation. Also, having had previous experience in insurance before taking a full time job means that they have a much better idea of what they're getting themselves into, and are more likely to stay.

Most carriers have internship programs which bring in college students to work for a summer or a semester to test the employee and give them some experience, in the hopes that they will come back for a full time position after graduation. Apprenticeship programs are less common.

An apprenticeship is a formal program that trains a person to do a specific job. Apprenticeships are aimed at people who already know which career path they're interested in and often involve signing a contract with the employer defining which skills they commit to learning. Apprenticeships can last from one to six years, and at the end, the employee not only has work experience, but they also get an official credential for it. Historically, apprenticeships were much more common in the skilled manual trades, such as electricians and plumbers, rather than in white collar work, like insurance. They have always been much more common in Europe than in the US, but it's a practice we should copy.

On the other hand, internships are short-term periods of temporary generalized work anywhere from a few weeks to a few months. Internships are useful to get work experience, test drive a company, and decide if it's an interesting career that you'll enjoy before committing long-term.[55]

In insurance, we found apprenticeships at Zurich, Lloyds, and a brand new one at The Hartford. Zurich's program started in their home office in Switzerland and has now been extended to their US headquarters in Schaumburg, Illinois. It includes on-the-job training and classes at a local college. At the end, completers receive an Associate in Applied Science in Business Administration. Currently, it has focuses on underwriting and claims. They are ramping up the program to have 100 apprentices by 2020.

The legendary Lloyd's launched their apprenticeship program in 2013, and it lasts 13 months, including two placements: one on the broker side and one on the managing agent side. The goal is to get a comprehensive understanding of Lloyd's working environment, underwriting, claims handling, and insurance broking. Completers receive an Advanced Apprenticeship in Providing

---

[55] Difference Between Internships & Apprenticeships - Chron

Financial Services and a qualification from the Chartered Insurance Institute (CII).

The Hartford's brand new program launched in 2017 and includes on-the-job learning along with classes at Capital Community College in Hartford or Rio Salado College in Phoenix. The program is two-years long, and completers are eligible for full time employment with the company along with an associate's degree.

Internship programs are much more common but vary immensely in quality. We chatted with students who interned at a variety of carriers and found that most didn't love the experience and were not convinced they would pursue a full time career in insurance once they graduated.

Most of the complaints we heard were that they were not challenged during the internship, that the projects they worked on didn't appear like they would have a real effect on the company, or that they didn't connect with the mission of the company and the industry. We believe strongly that a great internship is one of the best opportunities to bring in the brightest young talent and engage them in the industry.

Here are some suggestions on how to make your internship program awesome:

Work closely with the universities in your area so they get to know your company well and understand the type of students that are good matches for your culture. Career services staff at each school can have a huge effect on where kids choose to intern and whether they try to turn those internships into full time positions.

Just like with your new full time hires, a solid orientation program is key. You want to help them understand the opportunity ahead, how they will be measured, and what resources they'll have access to. It's also crucial to take this opportunity to help them fall in love with insurance. Remember, almost nobody grows up wanting to work in insurance, most of us fell into it by accident. This is the first (and maybe only) chance to share your story and help them understand how the industry does something good for the world, how your company is different, and to ignite in them the fire of love for the industry!

During orientation, be explicit in your expectations. Don't assume they know anything! Explain what time they should arrive in the morning and how late they're expected to stay. Make the dress code crystal clear. With a short-term employee, you just don't have time for a false start. Also set them up with a young full time team member who can serve as a buddy or mentor, a former intern who came back to work full time, and if possible, from the same area or the same school. Do everything you can to help them visualize themselves working there full time.

The biggest mistake you can make is failing to explain what you expect them to do and what goals you're going to hold them accountable for. Many interns show up and then spend weeks trying to figure out what they're supposed to be doing. They're bored, and many don't figure it out until their time at the company is almost over. An internship like this is worse than throwing money away. Not only did you pay them for doing very little, but you turned them off to the idea of coming back and taking a full time job at the company, or even in the industry overall.

Remind yourself every day that when the students go back to campus at the end of the internship, they will tell all their friends about interning at your company - whether they loved it or hated it. If they hated it, they'll probably tell not only their friends but also all their acquaintances! You can't afford to let them ruin your good name to future interns. Make sure you're giving them real work that has a real consequence for the company and that you make that explicit. The biggest thing interns are looking for (even more important than the paycheck) is real experience they can grow with and can use to impress in their interviews for real jobs. Getting coffee and making photocopies is not the kind of work that will send them back to campus excited to come back to work for you.

Given the small time frame you have with them, constant feedback and evaluation of the work is even more important. You should have a formal process of check-ins that happens at least weekly and corrects any problems right away. Mistakes should be addressed on the spot as they happen and shouldn't be kept in a file to be discussed at the weekly feedback session.

Give them tons of opportunities to network with the other interns and with the rest of the company. It is a lot of work to set up happy hours, baseball games, and other activities that make them feel like they're really part of the team, but it's worth it. In addition to making them feel like they're a part of the team, these kinds of activities will allow the interns to develop their networking skills. While we don't believe in making these activities mandatory, we do believe in explicitly teaching your interns the importance of networking and would go so far as to recommending a formal class on how to network appropriately at your company since this will vary depending on organizational culture. Insurance is and always has been a relationship oriented industry.

As the resident introvert, Carly struggled with how to network in a way that felt comfortable and authentic during her first few years on the carrier side of insurance. She spent time watching others and reading about it. Having a class that gave her strategies and direction would have been very valuable. Now that she has had a few years practice, she can even be seen out with Tony at conferences instead of in her room after the development sessions are over.

If all your intern did was work at the office, they didn't go back to campus feeling excited. The measurement for how good your internship program is should be the percentage of interns you gave full time offers to at the end of the internship, and most importantly, what percentage accepted. You should aim to have both measures at 90% or higher.

Many of the internship best practices above are adapted from this great article:
http://www.businessinsider.com/how-to-run-an-awesome-internship-program-2010-4

Chapter 15: Don't Overspecialize Entry Level Jobs

In previous chapters, we discussed how entry level jobs in insurance today are very different from entry level jobs of 20 or 30 years ago (where Boomers started their careers). This change has happened because of a stronger focus on controlling costs.

For example, on the claims side, many carriers figured out that handling all claims with field adjusters who needed a company car, laptop, cell phone, etc. was expensive and not very efficient. They found that adjusters would spend a good part of their day driving between clients instead of adjusting claims. It made sense to pull most claims adjusting into the office and do it over the phone, leaving only very complex claims to be handled in the field.

Once the claims teams had been moved into the office, they were able to handle a larger claims load since there was no longer time spent driving between customers. Then some carriers realized that while it is expensive to train a claims professional to handle multiple lines of coverage, you can handle claims more cost effectively if you have the employees specialize. Some adjusters will handle only auto claims, and others handle only property claims, and so on. A few carriers even took this to the extreme and separated different lines of coverage into different claims teams. Taken to the extreme, you end up with a small claim being handled by five or six different adjusters - the liability representative handles the recorded interview and liability decision; the material damages adjuster handles the auto damages; the first party medical adjuster handles the first party injury while the bodily injury adjuster handles the third party injury; and of course the injuries go to a whole new adjuster if the customer or the claimant get a lawyer involved!

This can significantly lower costs as claims adjusters who handle small pieces of a claim can be paid a lot less than an adjuster that handles multiple coverages or even multiple lines. The problem is that it becomes a boring job for the employee, and since they're not getting broad experience, they're not becoming well-rounded claims professionals (much less well rounded-insurance professionals) for the future.

Even though this level of specialization might make sense in the short-term to save on costs, it is really bad for employee development and engagement. An employee who does nothing but first party medical bills, for example, will probably be bored within six months and probably won't feel challenged to grow and learn new things after less than a year. On the other hand, an employee who handles multi-line claims from start to finish will likely continue to feel challenged for several years.

What it comes down to is that many entry level carrier jobs, especially at bigger carriers, have become so thin that most high schoolers could do them. This makes them very uninteresting after a few months and Millennials are unlikely to be engaged in such an environment. We must make entry level jobs challenging and varied enough that they can hold our attention for at least three years. Remember that Millennials have the most education of any generation in the workforce - starting them out with jobs that can be done by a high schooler doesn't make sense.

Glenn worked as a first party injury adjuster. After about six months, he was getting really bored of handling nothing but injuries. He saw little variety in his job and was basically just reviewing medical bills day after day with no end in sight. He was getting really frustrated because he was not learning how to become a better claims person or overall insurance person and just felt stuck.

Fortunately, he got some good advice and earned his AIC and CPCU. Within a few months, he was recruited away to a smaller carrier and took a job as a field adjuster handling every type of claim in his territory. This job allowed him to work on much more interesting things, with a lot of variety, a lot of autonomy, and constant growth. He is now committed not only to the insurance industry but also to staying in claims. After almost five years in that role, he is now interviewing for a headquarters manager level role in claims.

We understand that most insurance companies' expense ratios are higher than they ought to be, and there's a lot of pressure to lower them, but lowering short-term expense ratios by making entry level jobs less engaging for a young professional is a bad long-term strategy. If making entry level roles deeper and more broad is simply not an option, a good alternative would be to experiment with rotation programs which are discussed in Chapter 18.

Later on, once employees have had a chance to test different areas, then it makes sense to let them grow into more specialized roles where they can focus on becoming experts on something, but at that point they should have had a broad exposure and good general knowledge. Specialization shouldn't be an attempt to make jobs easier, it should be because the job is deep enough to warrant an expert.

Key point: Don't make the job easy, make it interesting!

Chapter 16: We Need to Talk About Your Call Centers

Tony started his career in insurance at the same place where most Millennials are starting theirs - in the call center. In his case, it was a Farm Bureau claims call center in their beautiful suburban campus in West Des Moines, Iowa. He didn't know it at the time, but he got really lucky. That call center was very well run by enlightened leaders who realized they were training the future leaders of the company.

As early as the interview, they told him that their call center was different than most. They understood that going forward, most of the new, young talent coming into the company would start in this department. They had been tasked with engaging and training those young professionals so that they would grow into being productive employees, not only during, but after their time in the call center.

They told him that they wanted him to spend two to three years in the call center, doing a great job, while at the same time learning as much as he could about the company, and the insurance industry in general. After that, he'd be expected to start applying for positions beyond the phones. The department also required everyone to get their Associate in General Insurance (AINS) and their Associate in Claims (AIC) within their first two years. Failure to comply with the educational requirement could lead to termination.

The way the call center functioned on a day by day basis was also quite engaging. They were trained well and supported in their efforts to grow their career (even when it meant time away from the phones for a class). The call center answered all first notice of loss calls for both personal and commercial lines claims, so it was not overly specialized. There was a lot of variety in the day-to-day work.

More complex claims would be assigned to claims specialists outside of the call center, and simple claims would remain with the call center representative to finish. This allowed the call center workers to be true claims representatives and gain solid claims experience while still answering incoming calls! This resulted in great customer service as roughly 40% of all calls were answered by the person ultimately handling the claim. The customers were happy and employees were able to grow.

Before we explain the way they measured performance, we want to give a quick primer on call centers for the benefit of those who have never worked in one directly. In most call centers, employees are required to be logged into the phone system whenever they're "on duty," and all time has to be accounted for. The phone generally has three settings: Available, After Call Work (ACW), and Unavailable. (It's been a few years since either of us have worked in a call center, so forgive us if the names are not quite exact, and they do vary between call centers.)

Whenever the phone is set to "Available" the system will route calls to an available employee. After the call, they'll probably need some time to finish documenting what they did during the call and finishing up any other administrative tasks required by management. While they're doing that, they put themselves on "ACW," which means they're actively working but not ready to take the next call. Finally, they have "Unavailable," which means they're away from their desk and can't take a call. For example, going to the bathroom. The goal is to maximize time in "Available," carefully control time in "ACW," and minimize time in "Unavailable."

Even the way performance was measured was not bad at all (for a call center). While they did measure the amount of time you spent on "ACW" and "Unavailable," it wasn't the main thing they cared about. To the best of Tony's knowledge, they didn't measure the dreaded "Time on Call" (which means average length of an individual phone call) that most call centers use as their main measure of productivity. The main thing that counted in this particular call center was the number of new claims you took and the percentage of those that you kept.

At the end of every week, management would send out a list of the top ten representatives that answered the most calls and kept the highest percentage of those calls. Tony was almost always in the top for both categories, and he enjoyed the friendly competition. Since the list only included the top ten, not the bottom few, employees weren't offended by it; it was a very positive thing. They also included a congratulatory mention of everyone who had passed an insurance designation test in their weekly newsletter. This mention reinforced the stated commitment to growing and developing the employees in the call center. It showed that management cared about their employees gaining knowledge of the insurance industry.

While at times it could get hectic, the overall environment of the Express Claims call center was very supportive of employee growth, and nobody seemed to hate the job. Looking back on it, now eight years later, most of the people Tony worked with in that call center are still in insurance, and none of them are still call center workers. Many stayed in claims. Many are still at the same company. Very few left the industry. That's a successful insurance call center in our book! It was such a great place that Tony was sad to leave when he got an offer for a better claims position at Nationwide, which ended his call center days.

Unfortunately, we would find out as we met many other young insurance professionals that great insurance call centers that focus on developing their people are rare. Most are simply awful places to work, and while nobody seems to be keeping statistics publically, anecdotally we have found twenty horror stories for every positive one.

This was the hardest chapter to research in this book because there is very little information published about insurance call centers. We wanted to include retention statistics for insurance call centers vs non-call center insurance positions, but we were not able to find any (we also haven't been able to find retention statistics for Millennials in insurance vs non-Millennials in insurance). We wanted to include numbers about how many of our Millennial insurance professionals in the overall industry are working in a call center environment, but again, no numbers seem to be published.

We searched all the traditional insurance magazines: Insurance Journal, Business Insurance, IA Magazine, Risk & Insurance, AM Best's Review, and Property Casualty 360 for both "call center" and the softer euphemism - "service center" - and couldn't find a single article mentioning how many insurance professionals work in call centers or a single story about what it's like to work in those call centers.

We also searched newer sources covering the industry, including Insurance Thought Leadership, Coverager, and embarrassingly enough, even our own InsNerds. We didn't find a single article about how many people work in insurance call centers or what it's like to work in them. To do our part to correct this problem, we published an abridged version of this chapter in early 2017 and it caused a massive response!

There are many conferences about insurance, and none seem to be talking about our call centers. We go to a variety of insurance conferences each year, and we keep tabs on many more, and we have never seen a session about call centers. It's almost as if those call centers didn't exist!

So, we have no numbers to share or analyze in this chapter. We're going completely on personal experience and anecdotal evidence from chatting with hundreds of young insurance professionals over the years and interviews specifically done for the book.

Our conclusion is that a huge, though unmeasured, portion of young insurance professionals in the 2010s started their insurance careers in a call center type environment. Most of them already had college degrees (and the associated student loans). Like previous generations, they fell into insurance by accident, but unlike previous generations, they won't stay out of loyalty and having found great careers. If we do our job right and engage them in the industry, they'll grow. If we don't, they'll leave the industry, and we'll forever continue having a huge talent gap.

We're not suggesting that we should close all the call centers and go back to doing this business exclusively in the old fashioned way. We understand that our expense ratio will not allow us to do that in the age of price transparency and incredible competition for every insurance customer. What we're suggesting is that we need to realize that in many cases the call center is our only touchpoint with the customer, and we should be making them love their time "with us." Also, the call centers are our new entry level point for new talent, and given the talent crisis, our less than stellar reputation with the general public, and the high expense of replacing any employee, we need that talent to grow with us.

Based on the horror stories we've collected from conversations with fellow young insurance professionals who survived some time in the call center and lived to tell the tale, here's what many (but not all) of the insurance call centers are like to work in:

Employees are required to be logged into the phones every minute they are in the office and are not allowed to even be in the office outside of their work hours. There are rows after rows of grey cubicles, packed with unhappy 25 year olds, college degrees hanging precariously from the cubicle wall, and the headset making a semi-permanent mark on their ear.

Engagement is so low, that it could better be measured on level of desperation. Turnover is high, with the great majority leaving not only the company, but the industry, and swearing they'll never work in insurance again. The representatives that haven't quite given up on the industry yet are applying desperately to any open entry level position that's not a call center. It doesn't matter if its claims, underwriting, processing, or subrogation. Anything will do just to get off of the phones! There's so many applying for the same jobs with essentially the same resume, college degree, and one to two years of insurance call center experience, that's it's very hard to differentiate among them, so hiring managers mostly just reject them without an interview. Some have been told directly "we don't hire from the call center." The person that told us during an interview about a hiring manager telling him that exact line was actually very thankful for the honesty. He's now an independent agent and very happy to have left the call center.

They are measured on 50+ different characteristics, so many that it's impossible to actually focus on improving. Who can control that many different minor factors during each phone call? The most important measures tend to be "Time-on-Call" and "Availability." The first one measures the length of their average call with the goal of keeping it as low as possible, and the second one measures the percentage of the time they're available to take calls. In some extreme cases, even mandatory team meetings count against them the same as time spent in the bathroom counts against them.

Performance evaluations are focused 100% on metrics and very little on growth or what is needed to do to get out of the call center. Most of the supervisors are former call center representatives themselves who only know the call center life and don't have an understanding of anything else about the company or the industry. They can't serve as good mentors even if they wanted to.

Professional development is encouraged by the company, but development time allowed by the department is very limited or completely non-existent, leaving it to the employee to do all growth activities outside of work hours. A case could be made that a motivated employee can grow by investing his own free time into activities, like insurance designations, Toastmasters, and networking, but most have no previous insurance experience and no advice on what they should be spending their time doing in order to grow with the company. The only thing they know is that they don't want to be on the phones, and they don't want to become call center supervisors either. They have no idea how to actually grow.

We have even heard stories of call center employees being denied support in getting their basic insurance designations because they're not required for the call center job they're doing. Some are denied even the ability to participate in activities such as Toastmasters or a young professional group because those meetings are in the office, and management doesn't want them to be in the office outside of their work hours.

We've had many Millennials complaining that this is what they usually hear from their managers. "Make sure to keep your time on call as low as possible. Your goal is no more than a 90 second average per call. Any time you're at the desk, stay logged into the phones, which will ring automatically. Document the call before hanging up because the next call will come right after you hang up. Put yourself on offline status to go to the bathroom or to meetings, but keep your offline time to less than 10% of your shift." Would you be able to provide great customer service, make the company look good, and develop yourself in that kind of environment?

There are better ways to run a call center. Not only should others learn from the example of Farm Bureau Financial Service and their Express Claims call center, mentioned earlier in the chapter, but there's even more that we can learn from the best ran call centers outside the industry.

Imagine if we could transition that conversation so that what Millennials in our call centers get told is more like this: "You're in the call center right now. I want you to do a good job here, but I don't want you to be here for more than two years. I want you to get your AINS. I want you to become involved in Toastmasters. In about six months, I want you to start networking within the company, finding areas you think might be interesting for your next position, and job shadowing in those areas. I want you to not only do well, I want you to do amazing, because if you do amazing I guarantee you're not only going to do well in this company, but in this industry."

We want to give you a guided tour of Zappos and what we think insurance companies should learn from them and the way they run their call centers.

Zappos was founded on the crazy idea of selling shoes online. Think about that. Shoes are the kind of thing that absolutely have to be tried on in person, and when you go shoe shopping, chances are you try multiple shoes before you find a pair that fits just right. Zappos succeeded selling shoes online by doing two things differently: They'll ship you as many shoes as you want and then you can try them and keep the ones you want, returning the rest. Zappos will cover the shipping both ways.

The second thing Zappos does, and what is most important for our purposes here, is provide amazing customer service. In order to provide that service, they run large call centers staffed by extremely happy employees. How do they keep call center employees happy? By doing things diametrically differently from most other call centers.

The hiring process consists of several interviews, and they're mostly hiring for personality fit. The HR representative conducting the first interview is tasked with simply figuring out if this is a person they would want to work next to for 40 hours a week. Skills are much less important as they can be taught. During the hiring process, Zappos makes it crystal clear that the great majority of positions at Zappos are at the call center, and if a candidate takes the job, they'll be answering the phones for a long time.

Every new employee, regardless of position, must go through call center training. Even a new Vice President will train in the call center with everybody else. After completing training, everyone gets to work the call center for a couple of weeks before moving on to the job they were hired for. This guarantees that everyone in leadership knows what the call center is like. Currently, in insurance, there are very few, if any, senior executives who came from the call center, partially because those call centers didn't exist or were much smaller when those executives were starting their careers.

After their first couple of weeks on the phone full time, all new employees get called into a huddle room with their manager. The conversation includes giving the employee real feedback, both positive and constructive, about their performance in the call center. Then the manager reminds them that most jobs at Zappos are at the call center level and that it's hard to move to a different area. Finally, the manager says something like, "Charlie, I've got a check in your name for $2,000. I want to pay you to quit. If you don't love the job, take the money, and we can part ways, no hard feelings." They do such a good job in hiring, orientation, and training that only 2% of people take the offer.

The way they measure performance is very different from other call centers too. They don't measure "Time-on-Call" at all. All they care about is making the customer happy. That could mean ordering a pizza for a customer who is traveling and doesn't know where to get a pizza from or chatting for seven hours with a customer about which shoes to buy for her upcoming prom.

Zappos understands that happy employees lead to happy customers. They understand that in a world where your only interaction with the customer is when they visit your website or call your call center, this is the only opportunity to connect with the customer. Zappos understands that a call center is NOT a cost center, it's their *only* touchpoint with their customer. What could be more important than that?

The insurance industry has a lot to learn from the Zappos way. As Millennials - who are not fans of visiting an agent's office - become a bigger and bigger part of our customer base, the call center becomes the *only* touchpoint to 95% of customers that didn't have a claim in any given year. Also, if the majority of your new young employees are starting at the call center level, it's the only chance of getting them to fall in love with the industry and to convince them to make it a career.

To learn more about the Zappos way we highly recommend the book *Delivering Happiness* by Tony Hsieh, the founder of Zappos. This amazing book will give you a great intro into how Zappos runs their business, especially their call centers. If you want to learn more, they also provide guided tours of their offices in Las Vegas. They provide training and consulting for other companies through their consulting arm, Zappos Insights. You can learn more at https://www.zapposinsights.com/ .

We are strong believers that the first large carrier to figure out how to turn their call centers into Talent Mines will have a major competitive advantage in the talent wars. Combine that with Student Loan Aid and opportunities to take Sabbaticals every few years (discussed in future chapters), and you'll create an unmatched employee experience that Millennials will not want to leave.

Chapter 17: Student Loan Reimbursement

Tony is a well paid underwriter at a major carrier, making very decent money, but he also has $100k of student loans that will probably take him 20 years of payments. The payments aren't trivial either. Using the Pay-As-You-Earn repayment plan, his payments in 2016 were $560 a month. Think about that for a moment. That's what some people pay for rent! That's half of the mortgage for a nice house.

Tony is not an exception to the rule. The average monthly student loan payments for recent grads are around $420, and for many it's $500, $1,000, or even more[56]. Fortunately, Tony managed to get both a bachelors and an MBA for his obscene student loans... he's one of the luckier ones!

Remember when tuition was $1,000 for the year, and you could work the summers to make enough money to pay for college without taking student loans? Millennials don't! But their parents have told them that those were the good old days.

It's no secret that Millennials are the most educated generation ever, but they are also the most indebted for that education. A few years back, we suggested adding student loan aid to the benefits package at a major carrier. We made the suggestion on Yammer,

---

[56] Student Loan Assistance: It attracts Millennial talent & keeps them in their seat

the company's in-house social network. The conversation immediately lit up and received wide support from Millennials who largely swore this would win their loyalty. Many of them called it a life changing idea! Not surprisingly, a few hours later, replies came complaining that it's unfair to help Millennials pay for their outsized student loans when they should have just worked through the summer to pay for the whole year of tuition and thereby avoided student loans.

While many Millennials worked evenings, weekends, and summers all through college, paying their full tuition out of pocket was simply not a possibility. The cost of college has increased by 6,900% for public schools and 5,100% for private schools. That's not a typo. Tuition has increased to more than five to seven times what it used to be in 1985[57]. In 1978, when today's 55 year olds were starting college, total tuition, room, and board at the average public university was just under $2,000. Minimum wage was $2.65 an hour, meaning it would take you 752 hours of work (not counting taxes) to pay for school for one year. By 2006, when today's 26 year olds were starting college, the total cost had risen to $ 11,034, while minimum wage had only grown to $5.15. It would've taken 2,142 hours of work (again not counting taxes). For most people, it became literally impossible to work their way through school to avoid student loans. In 1984, there was $35

[57] Life Delayed: The Impact of Student Debt on the Daily Lives of Young Americans

124

billion dollars in total outstanding student loan debt; today it's $1.2 trillion dollars[58].

One of Tony's very good friends started working at Nationwide full time in the mail room right after high school at the young age of 19. She took advantage of Nationwide's tuition reimbursement program and earned both her bachelors and master's degrees part time while also getting promoted several times out of the mail room, into a finance position, and most recently, into a very awesome middle level role. She was incredibly smart to go this route, and we should use her as an example for future generations as the smart way to pay for your college while getting real life work experience.

Unfortunately, most Millennials didn't get such great advice. Instead, they were generally told to follow their dreams, go to the best school possible (regardless of cost), study what they love, and give it their best. They were told they'd get a great salary once they graduated, and they believed it. Then, they graduated into the greatest economic recession in 80 years and found themselves to be over-educated, moderately-paid, low-level employees. Sadly, middle class salaries didn't inflate to match the five to seven times increase in tuition.

---

[58] Life Delayed: The Impact of Student Debt on the Lives of Young Americans

Most large companies generously offer $5,250 a year for "tuition reimbursement," which is good. Unfortunately, this can only be used to pay for tuition expenses incurred today, not to repay the tuition from a few years ago that allowed Millennials to get in the door with the company. This great benefit was designed for a generation where many came in without college degrees and used it to complete their education. Millennials in insurance largely are coming in with a bachelor's degree in hand, so this benefit is rather meaningless to them. To the carriers' benefit, a bachelor's degree has become the new high school degree. Take a look around your call center, and you'll find that most of your employees have a college degree already. For them, tuition reimbursement might mean getting a masters degree or a CPCU, but it doesn't alleviate their constant stress about paying for their existing student loans. They probably wouldn't be working at your company if they didn't already have a bachelor's!

We are not at all saying that a college education is a bad investment. Workers with a bachelor's degree earn 84% more over their lifetimes than high school graduates. They also have much lower unemployment[59]. For Millennials, college was a necessity, and for most of them, the student loans were inevitable.

Nothing beats the loyalty you'd get if you started allowing them to use the tuition reimbursement money to repay their existing

---

[59] Life Delayed: The Impact of Student Debt on the Lives of Young Americans

student loans, which after all were used to get them in the door. Would you have hired them without a degree? Nope, we didn't think so. Realistically, Millennials are not the only employees who would appreciate this benefit. Many Gen Xers still have student loans up for repayment, and Baby Boomers may have student loans if they were laid off during the recession and went back to further their education. In fact, 45% of Millennials surveyed said they would leave a job to get student loan aid[60]! That matches up almost perfectly with the 42% of Millennials that have college debt[61], meaning pretty much every Millennial with student loans would leave a job for this benefit.

We understand that current IRS regulation doesn't allow tax-preferred treatment of retroactive tuition reimbursement, but that doesn't mean it's impossible to provide the benefit. In the short-term, employers could simply do it in a taxed manner, giving their employees the $5,250 and retaining the taxes. They'd end up seeing something like $3,500 after taxes. Then, help them lobby for change to the tax code to get tax-preferred status in the future. Employees want to see the companies they work for supporting the causes that truly affect them; lobbying alongside them to get tax-preferred status for a valuable benefit would buy a lot of goodwill! The first large carrier to visibly support house bill

---

[60] State of the American Workforce - Gallup
[61] Student Debt Viewed as a Major Problem; Financial Considerations Important Factor for Most Millennials When Considering Whether to Pursue College - Harvard University

HR.795 - Employer Participation in Student Loan Assistance Act (or whatever future bill attempts to do this) - will have a *great* tool to recruit Millennials.

Employers could also consider making it contingent on performance, something like a bonus only given if the employee meets the requirements, and the check could be made directly to their student loan servicer. Employers could force repayment if an employee leaves the company within a year or two, similar to how tuition reimbursement is handled currently.

Sadly, as of 2015 only 3% of companies offered student loan aid, despite the fact the more than half of Millennials said they worry that they won't be able to repay their student loans[62].

Think about it a little more. It costs the company up to nine months of salary to replace an employee. So for a $50,000 salary, it costs close to $38,000[63]. This is based on a study from the Society for Human Resource Management (SHMR), but other studies have found numbers as high as two times their annual salary, especially for higher earning employees.

---

[62] Society for Human Resources Management - Student Loan Ais Attracts Millennials 2015

[63] https://www.zanebenefits.com/blog/bid/312123/employee-retention-the-real-cost-of-losing-an-employee

Companies are already offering tuition reimbursement money. Offering it in a way that most benefits their employees will save a ton of money in the long-term, differentiate companies in the hardening hiring market, and buy a much more engaged workforce that will not forget about what their employer did to help with their student loans. Do you want your Millennials worrying and distracted about how they're going to pay their bills, or do you want them fully engaged with being the very best insurance professionals they can be?

Research suggests that 90% of Millennials would be more willing to take a job offer at a new company if it offered student loan aid. Talk about a tool to go on the offense in the talent war! It will also help retain current employees as 94% have said that they would feel encouraged to stay at their current employer longer. Productivity would increase, stress would decline, they would have a more positive attitude, and be more committed[64].

There's a consultant at USI Insurance who recommends to her clients to start using student loan repayment assistance as both a recruiting tool and a retention tool. Sometimes she even recommends companies replace tuition reimbursement with student loan aid, if they can't afford to offer both[65]. This is how big of a deal this is! We never thought we'd be advocating ending a

[64] The Impact of Student Loan Benefits on Employees - SoFi
[65] Student Loan Repayment Could Be 2017's Hottest Employee Benefit

company's tuition reimbursement program, but if you must choose one, your new employee base would prefer student loan reimbursement. And, you would benefit by attracting a more educated workforce.

If you're thinking this is a temporary problem that affects a small set of Millennials who were unlucky enough to go through college with the worst possible timing, keep in mind that this problem is not getting smaller. Total student loan debt increased a massive 20% between 2008 and 2012[66]. That's one class of students. If you had two kids and one was a college freshman in 2008, he had to borrow $30,000 to get through school. If your second child started school in 2012, he would've had to borrow $36,000 to go to the same school. This problem is not getting any better. Companies must do something in order to keep their employees from being utterly distracted at work and vulnerable to being recruited away for a small raise just to help pay down their student loans.

In the last few years, multiple service providers have appeared to help with managing this benefit. Among the best known are Gradifi, Student Loan Genius, Tuition.io, and SoFi. Each company has their own angle, but ultimately, they all allow you to easily set up an employee benefit to contribute money paid directly to their student loan servicer and tie it to whatever requirements you decide. SoFi has an incredible white paper filled with information

---

[66] Policy Brief - The Student Loan Debt Review - February 2014

that is very eye opening. Student Loan genius has a very cool "Genius Match" feature that works very much like a 401(k) match where the company's payments are triggered when the employee makes payments to their student loans.

We believe that whichever insurance company starts offering student loan aid first will have a major advantage in the talent wars and will develop a loyalty from its Millennial employees that others can only dream of. A great place to start the discussion would be to add a couple of Millennials to your company's benefits committee. If they're not represented, the committee will continue to make decisions based on assumptions that all generations want and need the same benefits.

Student loans are such a burden on young employees, that many of them feel they can't start saving for retirement because of student loans[67]. The numbers are staggering with 62% of Millennials saying they put off saving for retirement because of student loans[68]. Imagine being in their shoes. You just started your career post-college. Your student loan payments are so high they're keeping you from buying a house, getting married, having kids, and saving for retirement. You understand that pensions are, for the most part, a distant memory now, and that you must use the company 401(k) to save for your own retirement. But you feel

[67] Student Loan Reimbursement Could be 2017's Hottest Employee Benefit
[68] Life Delayed: The Impact of Student Debt on the Daily Lives of Young Americans

131

you can't contribute to it because of your giant student loan payment. Would you be fully concentrated on your job with that worry in your mind? While employees still agree that 401(k) and healthcare are important, 89% of them believe companies should offer student loan repayment as part of their benefits[69].

Gaddafi offers an interesting option that allows employers to match employee's verified student loan payments with non-taxable contributions to their 401(k)s. This is downright genius because it avoids the problem of the payments being taxable!

It's not just retirement; 55% said it affected their ability to buy a home, and 21% are putting off marriage until they get their student loan situation under control. Forty-seven percent say that student loans are impeding their ability to grow in their careers[70]. These are not trivial numbers! Over half of student borrowers would prefer their employer help pay off student loans than provide health care or a 401(k) contribution[71].

Interestingly, student loan aid would help your diversity efforts. Women are 50% more likely to carry student loan debt than men, and they're 50% more likely to feel defeated by their debt[72]. Other

---

[69] Survey Finds Student Loan Reimbursement a Hot New Benefit for Job Seekers
[70] Life Delayed: The Impact of Student Debt on the Daily Lives of Young Americans
[71] These Companies Help Pay Off Their Employee's Student Loan Debt
[72] The Key to Attracting Millennials - Educational Assistance

minorities, such as African Americans, are also disproportionately affected. In 2013, 42% of African American families had student loans, a much higher percentage than the 28% of white families that did[73]. Given those numbers, it's easy to see how a student loan aid benefit would be a huge attractor to bringing and retaining more diversity in your company.

We know this is a brand new idea to most insurance companies, and that many of our readers are still thinking something along the lines of "these entitled Millennials, why didn't I skip this chapter?" But don't take our word for it. Even huge companies like Fidelity have jumped in on this benefit. Fidelity found that retirement benefits that have long been the cornerstone of benefits packages, even generous ones, did not resonate with their young employees. Fidelity's 401(k) plan is pretty amazing. If you contribute 7%, you receive a 7% match *and* profit-sharing can add another 10% on good years for a total 24% contribution. Even that plan wasn't perceived as a valuable benefit by their Millennials until they adopted student loan aid[74].

Here are some reactions from companies in other industries that have led the way. All quotes taken from tuition.io on March 29, 2017.

---

[73] The Disproportionate Burden of Student-Loan Debt on Minorities
[74] Medical, Dental, 401k? Now Add School Loan Aid Program

"When we made the announcement, it went around like wildfire [...] For the first time ever I was getting high fives in the hall. The reaction was so unique and unexpected."
-*Jennifer Hanson, Head of Associate Experience at Fidelity*

"Student loan debt is a ball and chain for young people, and is often a bigger priority than retirement [...] Like everything, you have to stand out to attract talent."
-*Christopher Webb, CEO at ChowNow*

"Our employees are thrilled with the program [...] It was only just implemented this year, and has already saved our team roughly 86 years in student loan payments."
-*Esther Lem, Chief Marketing Officer at Chegg*

Here are some quotes from students held back by student loans. Both quotes are from "Life Delayed: The Impact of Student Debt on the Lives of Daily Americans."

"I'm an educated, hardworking professional with a decent salary. At this point in my life, I wish I was saving for a house. But student loans are a huge burden; they're the new mortgage for many people in my generation."

"We both have excellent credit, and absolutely no debt other than student loans. We had set aside $7,000 to use as a down payment towards a home. But, we were denied a home loan because we 'simply had too much student loan debt.' "

While it is easy to name all the benefits of working in the insurance industry, and it can be easy to dismiss the student loan issue as a problem made by Millennial's own decisions, there is no question that financial anxiety distracts your employees from their work. Offering this benefit would pay dividends to your company and to your employees who are saddled with these loans.

Chapter 18: More (and Bigger) Rotation Programs

"Millennials believe that training is the best way employers can demonstrate an investment in them."
-Insurance Journal - Millennials Aspire to be Workplace Leaders; Seek Training

Development and rotation programs are very popular with Millennials. So much so that 41% would leave their job for a professional development program[75]. Part of the reason is that many of them are very structured which jives well with a generation raised with pre-arranged schedules of classes, sports, extracurriculars, and playdates. Millennials crave a higher level of structure while at the same time being allowed to be themselves. Rotation programs are a perfect match for Millennials' core workplace value of long-term career development and multiple experiences within a single organization. They allow them to "experiment and take risks as they figure out their niche.[76]"

When generational expert Cam Marston spoke at NAMIC's Annual Meeting in 2016, he talked about how Millennials are different, how to recruit them, and how to retain them. We'll talk more about his ideas around recruiting them in Chapter 22. He mentioned that Millennials have always had a syllabus, and they

---

[75] State of the American Workforce - Gallup
[76] Generational Talent Management for Insurance

crave that level of structure. That is one of the things that rotation programs can provide compared to the traditional entry level job. Let's look at an example:

Joe gets hired right out of college and begins his career at a large insurance carrier. He is an auto material damage in-office adjuster. He receives training on how to do auto claims and not much else. The first few months he learns a lot, but after about six months he starts getting bored. He's gotten pretty good at auto body damage claims, but he'd like more exposure to the rest of claims, recorded interviews, liability decisions, and the injury part of the claim. He starts looking at other jobs within the company and they seem interesting, but a coworker tells him that the company rule is that you can't apply for another job internally until you've been at your current position for 12 months.

"Six more months!? But I'm bored already..."

That's not a great start to his career. The company might get lucky, and he'll stick around until the 12th month and then find another claims role that won't bore him out in six months. However, they might not be so lucky, and he might again get bored when he gets to the next stop. Or he might just leave the industry.

In contrast, Dan started his career in a rotation program at a large carrier. The program had a one month orientation where he connected with many other new hires in the program and made some good friends.

After training, his first rotation was in auto damage claims where he worked for nine months. There was heavy emphasis in training and in becoming not only a good auto damage claims adjuster, but also in learning claims overall and insurance from a very broad level. Being well prepared for the next few rotations in claims was very important, and all members of the rotation program were required to take their AIC. Some went as far as starting to work on their SCLA (Society of Claims Law Associates) or CPCU. Management was very supportive of those efforts and spewed lots of praise on those who kept up their performance and earned extra designations. Towards the end, he was a bit bored and ready to try the next rotation, but he never got restless because he knew the next rotation was just around the corner.

His second rotation was in property claims which he enjoyed. It wasn't until his third rotation in injury claims that he fell in love. The casualty claims department did a great job in giving him access to the higher level claims reps handling interesting claims involving mediation and litigation. Towards the end of his third rotation, he applied to stay full time in that department, and they were happy to have him. He could have kept rotating through a few more areas before having to make up his mind, but having found where he felt at home, he was confident and ready to set down some roots.

A few carriers have rotation programs, most of which are specific to an area such as claims or underwriting rather than spending time in several areas. This is a good start, but for now, it means that the great majority of Millennials are coming into the industry through traditional entry level roles that tend to be much less engaging and don't do nearly as good of a job creating well rounded insurance professionals or getting them to commit to staying in the industry.

Rotation programs are a win/win/win in that they retain the more efficient cost structure of having specialized jobs rather than broad jobs, while at the same time molding well rounded insurance professionals and creating engagement. They also provide real opportunities for Millennials to "pay their dues" and get noticed. Millennials are much more likely than Boomers - 45% versus 18% - to say that a job that accelerates their professional development is "very important[77]."

Research from 2015 found that 77% of graduates in the US and 84% in the UK expect their employers to offer formal training

---

[77] Gallup's State of the American Workplace

programs[78]. The question is not whether you need a formal training program, the question is how long you can get away without one.

Talent Magnet talks about "a leading global carrier" who launched a development global leadership rotation program for its best recruits. (Our best guess is this is in reference to Swiss Re's Graduates Programme, but we could be wrong.) The program targets top graduates from leading schools around the world, and they are given 44 weeks of classroom and on-the-job training. They also get six weeks with the most experienced and inspirational company executives and an executive mentor. The program involves a "core placement" and two assignments in different countries with different functions.

Another example from *Talent Magnet* is a "leading US carrier" whose recruiting program is focused on partnering with top universities. They provide the ever important summer internships, and they make sure the interns work on "meaningful, mission-critical work." The students get to do three rotations in different areas of the business and interact with executives. This creates a pipeline of new workers who are ready to hit the ground running if they take a full time job with the company. The former interns also form an alumni network and build awareness on the campuses they focus on. The loyalty they create is so awesome

---

[78] Accenture - The Insurance Workforce of the Future

that a participant described how he felt, "I can't speak highly enough about my internship and the people. Now, I feel if I went to another company, I'd be letting myself down."[79]

Nationwide Insurance has two excellent programs that deserve mention and should be copied throughout the industry. The Financial Leadership Rotation Program (FLRP) and Marketing Leadership Rotation Program (MLRP).

Before we continue, a quick disclaimer: Tony is a graduate from Nationwide's FLRP. He's kind of an oddball graduate, since he didn't place into the Finance Department but rather went to Sales Management. However, he did spend a year in the program and had an amazing experience.

"The Finance Leadership Rotation Program (FLRP) is a rotation program designed to develop our next wave of financial leaders. The program consists of two to four cross-functional, cross-company rotations within the discipline of finance, investments, strategy, accounting, and internal audit. The program is intense and offers strategic rotation assignments in key business segments and corporate functions. It has been designed to develop and enhance leadership competencies required for the 21st century. Assignments are designed and prioritized by the top financial

---

[79] McKinsey & Company Talent Magnet

leaders from across the enterprise and are customized to meet the development goals and preferences of the participants."[80]

This intense program hits all the major things that a rotation program should cover and also provides its members with an Executive Mentor. It has built a strong alumni network within the company. The MLRP program is very similar, but participants rotate through marketing roles instead of finance.

Both programs feature a one month training and orientation that covers most of the things we suggested in Chapter 8, which creates real buy-in. After orientation, participants have the chance to work between two and four rotations, each six months long, each in different areas of the finance organization. During each rotation, they're expected to be full time contributing members of the the team while still participating in various FLRP activities, many of which are after regular business hours. They're also expected to actively network throughout the company, so they are able to find a permanent position at the end of the program, which is not guaranteed. The training they get is absolutely top notch with expert trainers brought in from some of the top training companies in the country. When Tony went through it, he participated in problem solving training by McKinsey & Company, Excel training by Wall Street Training, Public Speaking Training by the Harvard Theater School, Negotiation Training by

---

[80] Official FLRP job description during 2012-2013 when Tony went through it.

Karass, and multiple internal training sessions with executives from all over the company. It was truly an amazing experience.

We have only two complaints about the program: First, there should be a similar program dedicated to underwriting and another dedicated to claims since those are the core functions of an insurance carrier. Second, the programs usually only accept about 15 people total a year. Organizations need to find ways to scale up these types of programs!

Several other carriers have fantastic training programs that may or may not include rotations, but at a minimum include several months of a classroom training regime.

Here's a partial listing of some of the training programs we have heard about:

Zurich has training programs in multiple disciplines including Claims, Underwriting, Actuarial, Risk Engineering, and Finance[81].

CNA's well known Underwriting Trainee Program includes training both in the local offices and in their iconic red home office in downtown Chicago. Trainees get exposure to underwriting multiple lines of business as well as a formal mentoring program.

---

[81] https://www.zurichna.com/en/careers/training-programs

Travelers has an impressive array of opportunities with their "Leadership, Development, and Graduate Programs" in a variety of areas. Currently their website lists "Leadership Development Programs" in Actuarial and Analytics, Financial Management, Human Resources, Information Technology, and Insurance Operations. These programs are notable in that they are not just multi-month but two to five year long rotational programs. They feature rotations, cross-functional project work, and senior management mentors along with classes on both technical subjects and leadership. They also require that the participant be willing to relocate[82].

Travelers also offers "Development Programs" in Underwriting, Business Intelligence and Geospatial, Claims, Investments, Operating Model, Product Pricing, Technology Foundation, and Risk Control. These programs are shorter than the "Leadership Development Programs," most of them lasting only a few months, but they still offer the combination of classroom training, mentorship, and hands on experience in that function.

Keep in mind that 91% of employees who switched jobs also switched companies[83]! That's an organization's investment walking right out the door and into their competitor. If employees are going to change jobs anyway, why not make it easy for them

[82] https://careers.travelers.com/students-new-grads/development-programs
[83] Gallup - State of the American Workplace

to rotate internally, at least early in their career, in order to get their commitment and allow them to keep growing? A growing employee is an engaged employee, or at the very least, they're much more likely to be.

As reported in Deloitte's report, "Human Capital Trends in the Insurance Industry," Chubb found itself in a situation where 40% of their employees were retiring in the next three to five years. They also needed to find a way to attract and retain Millennials without increasing their training budget. That's no easy feat! They restructured their entire training department into a "hybrid model" where learning is managed at the department level but overseen by the training department. They introduced the very awesome idea of "pay it forward" to get subject matter experts to lead intermediate and advanced training. That is so fantastic! If companies can find a way to make this part of their culture, they're winning the talent war. The insurance industry has many employees with decades of institutional and technical insurance knowledge, and they're getting ready to walk out the door forever. At the same time, Millennials are feeling lost, have no clarity on how to grow, and aren't completely committed to the industry yet.

Chubb also introduced a Knowledge Management Department focused on gathering and documenting all that institutional knowledge before it walked out the door and invested in eLearning, gamification, peer-to-peer social media learning, and mentoring. We would love to read a book about these efforts!

Training and rotation programs like those we listed above are a fantastic way to come into the industry and provide a structured and much more solid way to grow in the industry. We encourage every carrier to learn from the existing programs and to design their own programs. These types of programs are a major advantage when you're recruiting for young talent. They help answer the ever important question, "How do I grow my career here?".

Chapter 19: A "Your Time Program"

Imagine an employee comes to you with a radical suggestion. She says something like, "I think we could leverage the relationships we have with our life insurance policyholders to sell a meal delivery service. We have all kinds of data on their health. We have an idea of their incomes and can guess, based on occupation information, which customers might not have time to go to the grocery store." What's your response?

Even at a truly innovative company, this type of suggestion might be met with skepticism, but if the company has a "Your Time Program," like Google, 3M, HP, and others, an appropriate response would be to send the employee off to do a proof of concept and share the results. Some everyday products from these companies are a direct result of these programs: PostIt Notes, Gmail, HTML. The details on the programs vary. They usually are set up to give employees somewhere between 10-20% of their scheduled hours to spend "tinkering."

We know that insurers must innovate to survive. A "Your Time Program" could lead to innovative suggestions from your existing employees. In addition, we would recommend allowing your employees to use this time to develop their skills and knowledge about their individual roles or the broader industry. Imagine your workforce devoted to pursuing designations or growing new services and products for your company.

To accomplish this, companies would need to build a culture and processes that supports "intrapreneurial" behavior. For most insurance companies, the biggest hurdles would be the following three issues:

1. Slack

For employees to take the time to innovate and grow, they must have workloads that allow free time. Allowing this time in their schedule will not only provide benefits to your company and customers, it will give your employees a feeling of direct ownership over a project or their own development. According to Gallup's 2017 *State of the American Workplace,* "42% of Millennials would leave a job to get paid time to work on a project of their choosing." Even if the project doesn't clearly tie back to insurance, the employment contract can be set up such that your company benefits from work done on company time.

For many production environments, like our service call centers or underwriting departments, it can be challenging to imagine giving employees time off the phone or away from their day to day duties, but it can pay dividends when done correctly.

Especially in call center jobs, with the current environment of efficiency and metrics, employees can feel like just a number. Organizations are treating them as though they don't trust them to manage their time, and as though their only value is in the hours they put in. While we recognize that call centers will never be replaced, we believe that this is the best place to find future talent, and nurturing that talent requires that we treat the employees in these roles as true knowledge workers. Companies should hire individuals who they believe have a long-term future in the industry. If they do this, these individuals will have the potential to improve organization's processes, services, or products during their "Your Time" hours. At the very least, they will use this time to pursue designations or education which will improve service to your customers.

One major challenge for Millennials who start their insurance careers in a call center is the directive from some HR departments that they are not to study for designations outside of work. A second challenge is that time off the phone can count against them in their performance assessments, so attending company sponsored professional development opportunities, like Associate Resource Group meetings or on site speaking sessions, can be discouraged. Building a "Your Time" Program would create built in time for these employees to develop professionally and contribute directly to the company on a project that is mutually beneficial.

Allowing your employees this time does necessitate a culture of trust. Hiring people who understand and have bought in to your mission is the only way to accomplish this. Your front line managers must be supportive of the program and rewarded when employees take advantage of it. In addition, your mission and culture must be engaging and front and center in all employee communications. Your employees must be on fire for your company.

3. Guts

This final component might be the most challenging to develop. It will take commitment to empower your employees in this manner, and a willingness to fail must exist. Organizations may find a small number of employees who abuse the program; there must be a procedure in place to terminate those employees swiftly. They will definitely have employees whose projects are not financially valuable; and while this is not ideal, we believe that the benefits of an empowered and committed workforce may supersede the need for financial gain from every "Your Time" project. Finally, employees may present an innovative idea that sounds good on paper, and organizations may implement their work, and it may fail. This will be a cost of attempting to innovate.

It must be accepted and built into the culture that failure of a project is a part of the process; an organization may choose to tinker further with the project or cut their losses, but unless their employee was truly negligent, they ought not be punished just because of a failed "Your Time" project. Learning to accept and grow from failure is a necessity in an innovative organization.

This type of program would demonstrate a true commitment to innovation and employee development. Both of these are valuable to Millennials. The company that leads with this program will have the pick of the smartest, most driven individuals.

Chapter 20: Long-Term the Real Estate Must Adapt

State Farm just opened a brand new gigantic building two blocks from Tony's apartment in Atlanta, and they're already starting construction on another one across the street. The building looks really nice from the outside. But we do wonder whether it makes sense to invest in real estate to house thousands of employees for 30 to 40 years. In just a few years, our workforce is going to be predominantly Millennials and Gen Zers, many of whom will give strong preference to flexible work options.

Older generations of employees felt safe and proud to be working for a company with gigantic buildings, and we have to agree that CNA's red tower in Chicago is pretty cool looking (Tony adores red). But Millennials care much more about flexibility and how well the job fits their lifestyles than whether the company has a few giant buildings in town.

As we move towards a business world that accepts telecommuting, and as location independent jobs become commonplace, the goal of our office buildings should be to engage employees that *want* to come in a few days a week, even though they could work from home, Starbucks, or right by the pool in Jamaica. What would such a building look like? We believe the following trends will be important to the buildings of the future:

1. Less Square Footage Necessary

Twenty-first century knowledge workers have already begun taking advantage of the ability to connect to the office from anywhere that they can connect to the Internet. As we will discuss in Chapter 21, we believe this trend will continue to increase. This will lead to fewer workers requiring assigned spaces in the office. We expect to see practices like hoteling and hot desking increase in popularity due to this trend. Though we sometimes forget, there will always be workers who like to come into the office; flexibility will be key, so most likely, office buildings will never become fully obsolete. The necessity of having a desk for each individual employee will disappear and allow companies to invest capital in technology or education as opposed to physical buildings. However, buildings will need to be designed with remote workers in mind. Conference rooms ought to be built for tele-meetings, and spaces will need to be easily navigable to those who come into the office only once or twice per year.

2. Egalitarian Cultures

Most insurance companies are still quite traditional and hierarchical. This is reflected not only in their organization charts, but in the layout of their offices as well. Walk into any department, and you will probably see rows of cubicles, some larger than others, and offices around the perimeter of the office. The larger cubicles are for your front line managers and middle managers are in the offices. Your executives are on a separate floor and have traditional large offices. Though the layouts are traditional, many departments are moving towards a more modern culture and encourage managers to be accessible to employees. You often hear, "We have an open door policy here. Please stop by anytime." A fantastic way to reinforce that message is to arrange the office in a less traditional fashion. There are many options to consider.

Understanding how much collaboration ought to happen and how open office layouts impact employees' productivity, depending on the type of work they do, is a good place to start in making that decision. Open office layouts have been popular recently, but they must be built intentionally with space for focused work. As the introvert on our team, Carly would argue that even cubicles as they currently exist in most carrier offices make focused work challenging, as they are not private, and sound still carries throughout the floor. Providing conference rooms and focus spaces for your employees can be a great way to offset some of the challenges of open environments.

3. The Third Space

Much has been made of the potential for employees to work remotely. There will always be a subset of people who prefer to come in to the office, and there will always be some need for employees to gather in the same location. Many tech companies have dealt with this by incorporating a "Third Space" feeling into their campuses. The Third Space is a concept introduced by Russian psychologist, Lev Vygotsky. It refers to a place that a person feels almost as comfortable as they do at home or in their office. This has been incorporated into campuses through the creation of fun spaces, like slides in the office, music rooms, or ping pong tables. Cafeterias, laundry facilities, gyms, and day care centers also contribute to this feeling. If your offices are comfortable and provide daily services, your employees may feel more inclined to work out of the office than remotely.

4. Investments in Education

Finally, physical real estate will be necessary for hands on training. Some carriers already have facilities that can be used to train adjusters and risk managers about building materials, safety procedures, and best practices. We believe that more space ought to be devoted to these types of activities, and if an organization finds itself with office space not being used, they may have the perfect opportunity to adapt the space in this way.

Overall, the importance of physical real estate will decrease over time. Millennials and Gen Zers will value flexibility and will not be impressed by a brand new building, as they will see it as a sign that the company is tied to a single location.

Chapter 21: Flexibility Must Become the New Norm

"If you can't trust your employees to work flexibly, why hire them in the first place? A flexible approach to work also helps businesses retain their best talent as they are giving their employees an option to do great work, but in a way that fits their lifestyles, providing a win-win scenario for all. "
-Adam Henderson, Employee Engagement Consultant at The Millennial Mindset[84]

Carly and Tony both love their work from home days. Carly gets to work from home twice a week and Tony once a week. This has been a major improvement to their engagement, and their overall lives, compared to their first several years in the industry (when they had no ability to work from home at all).

We are not alone. Research has found that 51% of employees would leave a job to get more flexible schedules and work-from-home opportunities. The numbers are truly astounding; 96% of all employees (not just Millennials) said that flexible working is important[85]. Fifty-eight percent of Millennials rank a flexible schedule as a top benefit they want[86].

---

[84] https://www.linkedin.com/pulse/do-you-understand-millennial-mindset-adam-henderson
[85] Gallup's State of the American Workforce
[86] 2014 The Hartford Millennials Survey

We have been working on the topic of Millennials in insurance for five years. When we finally jumped wholeheartedly into writing this book, one of the most interesting things we discovered is that older Millennials like us, born in 1986 and 1982 respectively, view flexibility as a nice perk, but not an absolute must have. We imagined the younger Millennials who are graduating college today, born around 1993, would feel the same about work from home opportunities. Oh boy, were we ever wrong! The more we dug into the research for this chapter, the more we discovered that younger Millennials simply don't understand the need to go to into the office, and they see it as a major inconvenience! They are willing to come in for training, team meetings, and other times when it makes sense, but once they're up and going, they're not willing to have to come in four or five times a week.

The newest research indicates that the absolute best thing an employer can do to engage your Millennials is provide as much flexibility as possible in their work hours and allow them to work wherever they want to work from. We know this is scary, but soon it will simply not be an option; they will leave and go to work in other industries that are ready to provide them the flexibility they crave. Remember, by 2020, Millennials will make up 50% of the workforce!

We get it. After all, we *have* the technological tools to allow people to be productive regardless of location. We're not advocating letting them work from home right away, but once they're trained, and they have shown you they are mature and motivated enough to get their work done, why not?

Gallup also found that employee engagement, which strongly predicts productivity, increases as flexibility in working location does. "The optimal engagement boost occurs when employees spend 60% to 80% of their time working off site." So the sweet spot appears to be three to four days a week working from wherever they want, and one to two days a week working from the office.[87]

Surveys of insurance professionals are finding that 70% of full time workers between 18 and 29 want to work from home[88]. Jacobson Group's 2016 Insurance Industry Talent Trends reports that those who have the ability to work from home report being 73% happier. Happier employees treat your customers better and are more productive!

In the US already, 30 million professionals work from home at least once a week, and that number is expected to grow by 63% by

[87] Gallup's State of the American Workforce
[88] CanadianBusiness.com *70% of Millennials Workers Would Rather Telecommute*

2020. Not only that but companies can save around $11,000 a year for each person they let work from home.[89]

Right now many of our readers are thinking, "but you can't let a call center employee work from home, that doesn't make any sense." Well, you can and other companies do it! Our favorite example is Jet Blue.

Jet Blue's 800 strong reservations virtual call center is exactly that, virtual. Every one of the employees work from home! Those 800 employees *are* the reservation system. There is no backup. "When you call 1-800-JetBlue, you're going to get someone in their home," said their CEO, David Neeleman, to CBS News. The agents handle more than ten million calls a year and are 25% more productive than the old traditional call center which is now closed.[90] If Jet Blue can pull it off for something as stressful as an airline, there's simply no reason we couldn't do the same in insurance!

Gallup makes a better case than we ever could in their 2016 State of the American Workforce:

"Gallup has consistently found that flexible scheduling and work-from-home opportunities play a major role in an employee's

---

[89] 2016 Insurance Industry Talent Trends - Jacobson
[90] Jet Blue's Stay-At-Home Work Force

decision to take or leave a job. [...] Increasingly, people want to be able to adjust their hours and schedules and work remotely when they can without compromising quality or productivity. [...] The most meaningful [benefits] aren't rock climbing walls and unlimited beverages. The benefits and perks that employees truly care about are those that offer them greater flexibility, autonomy, and the ability to lead a better life."

The 2014 Hartford Millennials Survey found that "the current level of flexibility is not consistent with Millennial's desires. Eighty-eight percent wish they could, within certain limits, have greater opportunity to start and finish work at the times they choose. Seventy-seven percent wish for greater mobile connectivity. And the greatest gap is in working remotely, where 75% want to do it more frequently, and only 43% currently have the ability to do so."

Flexible work doesn't end with working from home. Once organizations perfect their work from home program and realize that their people are just as productive (or more), happier, and more loyal, they'll realize that, in most positions, there's little difference between letting them work from home and letting them go winter in Arizona.

Some roles that require frequent in-person contact are obviously going to still require employees to live near a particular geography. However, if 90% of a job is done using technology, does it really make sense to for the employee to show up most days (or even at all)? Once they're no longer required to be in the office, does it make sense to force them to still live nearby? Remember, soon over half of the employee workforce will be part of a generation that has very little patience for things that simply don't make sense.

Some carriers like USAA and State Auto have been making waves by experimenting with more and more work from home opportunities, but it's still not very common. We predict that the first carrier to rip off the Band-Aid and allow most employees to work from home whenever they want is going to reap significant benefits in terms of increased productivity, lower turnover, and financial savings due to decreased real estate costs. It would quickly become one of the most sought after employers in the industry, and this will give it a competitive advantage.

There are multiple other ways that jobs can become more flexible, and more attractive to candidates and employees. Amazon is testing letting some teams work 30 hours a week at 75% the pay of working full time, without losing benefits[91]. The 40 hour workweek is pretty arbitrary; it was created in the early 1900s to protect factory workers from being overworked and exploited[92].

---

[91] Forbes - *Amazon Experiments With 30 Hour Workweek*
[92] Wikipedia - Francis Perkins

This optional shorter workweek helps avoid burnout, allows new parents to be more present for their children, keeps workers focused[93], and is likely to become a huge hit with Millennials who can afford to do it.

Now that we've covered the basics: hours, work from home, and location independent jobs, let's turn our attention to something even crazier but that would gain your company incredible loyalty from some of your Millennials - sabbaticals. Long a staple of the academic world, sabbaticals have started bleeding over into the business world. Taking an extended period of time off, with lowered pay or no pay, is a difficult thing to sell, but it has many advantages. We are now seeing companies offering options like working nine months of the year followed by three months off (unpaid). Then there is the more creative four years of work at 80% pay followed by a one year sabbatical at 80% pay. Essentially, it becomes an automated savings plan for the employee's sabbatical, and they're guaranteed their job back when they return, taking the two biggest stressors that keep people from pursuing their long-term travel dreams off of the table.

Deloitte offers the option for a one month sabbatical after only six months of employment, or up to six months after two years at the company. General Mills offers 12 weeks sabbatical after seven years at the company. Perkins Coie allows up to three months of

---

93 https://hbr.org/2007/07/the-making-of-an-expert

sabbatical after ten years. St. Jude's Children's Research Hospital offers six to 12 month sabbaticals with between 50% and 100% of pay after five years. VMWare gives three month sabbaticals every five years[94].

There's a long list of companies that offer this amazing benefit: http://yoursabbatical.com/learn/workplaces-for-sabbaticals/ . The only P&C Insurance company or agency that we have found offering sabbaticals is NRG, a Seattle based agency. Good job leading by example!

Overall, we are big believers that the first large carrier to offer both Student Loan Aid (Chapter 17) and some sort of sabbatical option will become the employer of choice for many of the Millennials in our industry, and they will be *very* loyal employees.

We'll finish this chapter with a quote that we feel really summarizes the chapter:

"Work-at-home and flexible work options are becoming increasingly popular retention tools. As the labor market tightens and recruitment becomes more challenging, flexible work is a great opportunity to expand the talent pool."
-Catherine Prete, SVP of Operations at Jacobson Group[95]

---

[94] http://fortune.com/2015/03/16/paid-sabbaticals/
[95] 2016 Insurance Industry Talent Trends - Jacobson Group

Chapter 22: Recruiting Millennials

Recruiting - essentially this comes down to matching the right person with the right role and the right culture.

"People make decisions based on both reason and emotion, but they are more likely led by emotion. Therefore, organizations should clearly present how candidates can contribute to a role and organization."
-State of the American Workforce - Gallup

It might seem weird that this wasn't the first chapter in the book, but we think it's less urgent. We already do a decent job of bringing in thousands of Millennials every year into insurance, the bigger problem is keeping them. That's why we focused the book on the engaging and retaining side. But once we have the leaky funnel fixed it's time to focus on bringing in more, and better, quality talent into the industry.

To maximize the recruiting of Millennials, organizations have to go where they're at, and they are most certainly not reading the classifieds in your local paper! They are all over social media. Which social network is hard to predict because whether we tell you to hit Pinterest or Snapchat, by the time the ink is dry, that advice will be outdated.

Here's what companies can do: Hire a 22 year old intern. Get him to understand what the jobs you need to fill are all about. If they can't explain it to him well enough, they need to simplify the language (check out InsNerds.com Simplest Insurance Glossary). Now, let him post it all over the social media channels he's using today. Let him describe the job in his own words. Yeah, we're not joking. That's how to maximize reach.

The job posting itself is very important. Insurance positions, even entry level ones, are famously hard to figure out, especially by the very people we want to encourage to apply for them! How is a Millennial who didn't study Risk Management and Insurance (which makes up 85% of our new applicants) supposed to understand the duties of a job when its description is packed full of words that aren't used in general society, like "claim," "underwriter," "producer," or "medpay." Even graduates with a business degree, the great majority of which were not required to take an RMI class, will be confused.

Organizations should try to describe the job in the simplest possible terms, without using any jargon, and describe not only what the job actually entails, but also the characteristics of the people who are generally successful in this role.

For example, here's an actual job posting from a major agency:

"Responsibilities:

As an Agency Producer, you will support the sales, cross-sell, customer retention, and customer service goals of the Insurance Agency. You will do so by calling on prospective clients and generating new sales leads while also developing a deeper relationship with existing customer accounts. Leads will be provided to you, but you will also work to generate warmer sales leads through your own personal networking and prospecting.

Job Functions:

Utilizing Agency marketing systems, or those you may develop, to solicit and sell insurance and related products

Coordinating with the agent and/or operations manager to provide assistance in determining proper coverage

Providing excellent customer service to policyholders

Attending networking and/or community events

Educating and assisting customers

Maintaining knowledge of new products and initiatives

Pursuing a program for development of personal and business skills"

Now, here's a re-written version:

"Do you thrive on competition? Does seeing your name at the top of a list make your day? Are you the type of person who makes small talk with others in a queue? Are you excited to learn about others' lives?

If you answered 'yes' to these questions, an insurance sales position at Jones Agency might be right for you. We challenge our producers to meet stretch goals on a daily basis. Our producers are paid based on their results and have the opportunity to earn special bonuses if they outperform their peers."

Here's a second example from an actual posting:

"Responsibilities:

Analyzes commercial lines accounts to make decisions based on individual risk characteristics, exposure analysis, hazard recognition, and controls. Utilizes underwriting guidelines and company best practices to ensure compliance with state regulations. Within delegated authority levels and continuous process improvement work principles, accepts, rejects, or modifies new and renewal business to ensure a profitable book of business.

Prices business according to Company underwriting and pricing guidelines. Ability to use creativity and underwriting knowledge to write risks and retain business.

Partners with Territory Managers to support marketing activities by developing ongoing relationships with agents to discuss market appetite, quality, and profitability of submissions, service standards, and underwriting and/or product changes.

Communicates with agents on underwriting issues including, but not limited to, decisions on cancellations, declinations, exposure concerns, and survey results.

Partners with Territory Managers to identify issues or patterns and works to resolve or improve them; participates in agency planning and review processes; and may identify sales and marketing opportunities.

Travels, with or without Territory Manager, to assigned agent locations to develop agency partnerships.

Trains and educates agency staff in company products, services and underwriting philosophy.

Promotes the company's product and services by speaking to agent or insurance-related groups, and by networking within the insurance community to stay abreast of changes within the industry.

Actively participates in problem solving activities to define problems, assess current state root causes, design and test solutions, implement solutions, and sustain and continuously improve to permanently eliminate problems.

Actively participates in continuous improvement by fully engaging in daily huddles, generating suggestions, following appropriate procedures and continuous process improvement work principles, participating in problem solving activities, and utilizing continuous improvement tools to support the work of the team.

Performs other duties as assigned."

Compare that to this rewritten version:

"Do your friends rely on you to know the answers to their random questions? Is one of your catchphrases, "Let me Google that!"? When you're out and about, do you notice unsafe conditions or people taking unnecessary risks?

At XYZ Company, our underwriters are encouraged to do their homework. They serve as an advisor to producers and make million dollar decisions on behalf of the company every day. In this role, it is essential to have a thirst for knowledge and a love of research. Beyond that, the ability to explain complex or abstract concepts is a necessity."

One final example:

"JOB DESCRIPTION

Exercises independent judgment in the investigation, negotiation, and disposition of general liability, property and auto claims within limitations of authority in the client contract and according to claims handling instructions within the contract

Promptly investigates, evaluates, negotiates, settles and/or resolves claims and losses

Reviews the loss notice and policy to verify coverage, deductibles, loss payee/mortgagees, and confirms that the loss date falls within the coverage period

Takes statements from clients/claimants/employees/witnesses

Sets adequate reserves to cover company and client exposure-probable ultimate cost reserving

Communicates with clients/claimants/attorneys to negotiate the settlement of claims and losses

Issues payments within check authority limit"

Our rewritten version:

"Are you the friend who always knows just what to say in a difficult situation? Do you enjoy making things right? Do you have a passion for helping those in need?

If your biggest thrill comes from solving problems or putting a smile on another's face, you'll fit right in with the adjusters at ABC Company. Our number one goal is to get our insured's back to where they started after a claim. Our adjusters deliver that promise every day."

Better job descriptions directly relate insurance functions to the candidate's everyday life in a fun and easygoing way. The prospective candidate can see themselves succeeding at these actions, and their interest will be piqued. They'll wonder how a staid old insurance company will provide these types of experience on a daily basis. Once the job description has them curious, companies will be able to tell them all about their culture and ideals which will open their eyes to the wonderful possibilities of an insurance career. These are just examples we developed, but don't be afraid to ask existing Millennial employees in those areas to help come up with fun job descriptions for their jobs!

Rewrite entry level job postings in terms that your neighbor's 20 year old, who doesn't have a driver's license, because she uses Uber, can understand. If she can't explain it back in her own words, it's too complicated. Also, don't take it too seriously. Include a joke (even a bad one), or even have the 20 year old make a meme for the posting.

The Center for Generational Kinetics has done a lot of research on what to show in a job posting, so we include a summary of their findings: Organizations need to show that the job and the company are fun, challenging, creative, and that there is a big opportunity for career growth. Make the types of challenges they'll face in the first year explicit; preferably the first week, first month, and first year all spelled out. Make it clear that creativity is rewarded and that they'll have space to be creative. Making the opportunity for growth explicit is pretty easy by simply telling them about the demographic and talent crisis and how stable this industry is. Spend a good amount of the company description part of the posting talking about how the company helps its community and helps make the world a better place. Highlight any opportunities for intra-company entrepreneurship. Make it clear that diversity is embraced and that they're free to bring their whole selves to work. Then, finish it with a mention of flexible schedules and work life balance (even if they must successfully hit some benchmarks, like six months in the office first, it can be used as a carrot). The most important thing that a good job description must have in the posting is a good explanation of the company's mission in simple terms, and again, how it's making the world a better place.

All the efforts to attract Millennials to the industry and get them to check out a job posting are moot unless companies can get them to put in an application. An application system has to first be mobile, since 85% of Millennials access the web from their phones[96]. If a Millennial can't easily put in an application from their iPhone or Android in less than 15 minutes without getting confused or frustrated, it's costing you candidates. Honestly, we haven't found one insurance carrier with a decent job application system. We need to do better! Brownie points for allowing them to apply directly from LinkedIn without having to actually write an actual resume. All their info is on LinkedIn anyway.

One major mistake we have seen some carriers making is setting the wrong incentives for the recruiting team. If your recruiters are

---

[96] Gallup How Millennials Want to Work and Live

evaluated and paid on filling jobs quickly, and there is no long-term incentive for them to make sure they put the right person in the right job, they will try to shoehorn employees into whatever roles they to need to fill at the time instead of working to find them a role that's the right personality and skill fit. Recruiters should be measured and incentivized with long-term measures, like how long the Millennials they recruit stay in the company, how well they do in reviews, and whether they get promoted. Organizations need to encourage their recruiting teams to think long-term!

It's also important to realize that Millennials can smell marketing a mile away. Remove any stock photos from your careers website; it feels fake and makes them wonder why employees aren't happy enough to use their real photos.

Incorporate video where possible, especially video of existing Millennials talking about why they love the company and the job. Be careful of making the production quality too professional because it can feel like marketing. We're going for authentic, shaky camera and all!

Once you're ready to offer the job, *Y Size* recommends a specific way to do it, and we fully endorse it. Call them first and offer them the job, then immediately send them an offer letter, printed on fancy paper and delivered via FedEx. Make them feel special!

174

This gives them something tangible to show their mom so she'll believe it when they tell her they're moving out of the basement soon! Finish the deal by detailing three potential career paths that can start from the job offering, and some advice on how to grow towards those career paths.

Ariel graduated college with an accounting degree in 2010, right in the heart of the Great Recession; there were no jobs. She was recruited into a major carrier by an in-house recruiter and offered a position in a processing center. She was told by the recruiter that they did not have any open accounting positions, but that they would start her in a processing job and would move her over to accounting once a position became available. Time passed, and Ariel withered away in a lowly paid position that didn't really require a college degree. The call from the recruiter to move her over to the promised accounting role never came. Her calls and emails to the recruiter to check on the status of the transition went unanswered. After two years, she was so disillusioned that she quit and took a job outside the industry, swearing never again to work in insurance again.

These kind of stories happen because of misaligned incentives. Recruiters are under pressure to fill specific roles quickly, and have no skin in the game 30 seconds after the recruit arrives in orientation. Recruiters should be evaluated on the speed with which they fill a role, but also on how long the person lasts in that role and with the company. They should be getting a bonus every time somebody they recruited completes another year in the company, and when any of their recruits get promoted. This would encourage the kind of long-term thinking that we need from them; it aligns their interests with those of the recruit and the company.

We had the pleasure of virtually watching generational expert Cam Marston at the 2016 NAMIC Annual Convention via their amazing Connect Differently feature (which allowed us to watch the conference online). We were already big fans of Mr. Marston's work, but it was awesome to see him talking about the insurance industry! One of the points that really hit home for us was his explanation about how to recruit Millennials.

Baby Boomers are very attracted to stability and are very brand loyal. Millennials like stability, but they're more concerned about their own career growth potential and are not as brand loyal. Companies are used to recruiting new employees selling things like, "Diamond Re has been the reinsurer of choice since 1870. Our world-leading reputation for excellence extends from our A+ rating to our 120 year old headquarters office located in Berlin, Germany. We offer competitive salaries and benefits. Come see what it is like to work for a renowned industry leader."

That kind of offering of history, brand name, and stability was very attractive to Baby Boomers, but it's not effective for Millennials. Mr. Marston explained that for Millennials you must focus on their needs and their future, not on the firm, and the owner's history and background.

This might work better: "Platinum Re offers exciting and challenging careers. During your first 90 days, you will be trained on how to become a world class reinsurance underwriter, preparing to help the best carriers all over the world with their reinsurance needs. You will be assigned an executive mentor who will help assure your successful transition from college to the insurance and reinsurance industry. We will groom you into success you never dreamed possible." We love his approach and think it would be a much more successful way to get Millennials interested in insurance. (Diamond Re and Platinum Re are fictional companies we created to use as examples).

One final thing about recruiting Millennials. After doing the tactical work of writing a Millennial friendly job description and making sure to have a great mobile-first application system, it's time to sow the seeds for a good future harvest. Companies should grow their applicant pool for the future. Once they've followed our advice in this book, and Millennials who started in the last few months are super engaged, the first thing they need to do is to encourage them to invite their friends to apply. That's the low hanging fruit.

Carly has friends outside the insurance industry who don't understand her commitment to it. They often ask her why she spends so much time writing and thinking about insurance. However, many of them are unhappy in their current jobs. From time to time, she suggests that they consider the industry. Their responses are often something like, "I don't want to sit behind a desk all day" or "paperwork is boring." When she uses Mr. Marston's advice and explains the job in a way that speaks to each friend's individual strengths, she gets much better results. For instance, she has almost convinced one friend to look for a loss control specialist role by explaining that you get to spend your days inspecting companies and helping them improve safety for their workers and the community. She has another friend who would be perfect in an IT role at a major carrier, and she explains the issues they could see in transitioning from legacy systems because she knows that this friend truly enjoys being challenged.

We all need to invest in improving the image of the industry, and that's a long-term game. It is important to support organizations like InVest, InsureMyPath, and InsNerds, so the industry can continue recruiting young talent and helping them grow. Also, support Gamma Iota Sigma, the Risk Management and Insurance

Fraternity, as they do great work for the industry at the college level.

Chapter 23: Gamification

Most of this chapter is based on the excellent *Reality is Broken*, a book by Jane McGonigal, PhD. If we pique your interest in gamification, we recommend you begin your research reading that book. Anything in quotes or any number without another source comes from this book. Numbers or stories from other sources are footnoted. This book was written in 2011, so to avoid saying "back in 2011" several times during this chapter, all numbers are from 2011 unless otherwise sourced.

Tony and Carly are both gamers, though Tony is a much bigger gamer than Carly. Right now, you might be looking at our picture in the back cover (or on our LinkedIn pages) and wondering, "Didn't I read that they're both in their 30s? Have I been reading a book by two children?" Video games stopped being the kingdom of children when the Atari, Nintendo, and Playstation generation grew up and never quit playing their games. You might be surprised to learn that today the average gamer is 35 years old and has been playing games for 12 years! At this point, it's a part of who they are, and they are not going to stop!

If there are 1,000 Millennials in a company, they probably have 500 gamers of one kind or another. They range in gamer-ness (we probably just made up that word) from Tom in IT who is an avid World of Warcraft gamer and puts 60 hours a week into his obsession, to Nicole in Underwriting who loves her Candy Crush Saga. Tom is a proud gamer with an active Steam account while Nicole doesn't think of herself as a gamer at all. However, they are both avid game players. By 2011, in the US alone, there were 183 million active gamers (who report playing games regularly and on average 13 hours each week) and you can bet that this number has only grown since then. Tom counts as a an extreme gamer, that plays for more than 45 hours a week. You might think of him as an addict, maybe even a giant loser and wondering how you hired him, but you haven't noticed his low productivity at work. The reality is his productivity is probably fine, and there are some five million extreme gamers like him in the US (so chances are a few of them work for you).

People play games for multiple reasons, and research by Dr. McGonigal has taught us a lot. Gamers get a sense of being alive, productive, focused, and engaged in the moment from games that they don't get anywhere else in their lives, especially not in their day jobs. But it doesn't have to be that way! Over time, many of the features of gaming can be incorporated into jobs, and Millennial employees will start loving their jobs (if it's done right). It's one of the most powerful long-term investments to make into creating engaging jobs.

Worldwide, video games generated $91 billion dollars in revenues in 2016[97], more than twice as much as Hollywood's $38.6 billion dollars[98]. That's right, gaming is a bigger business than the movie industry. A much bigger business…

While about half of the population thinks of gaming as a clear waste of time (Tony's otherwise perfect girlfriend included), the techniques that games have developed and perfected to keep people hooked can be utilized for productive purposes!

"Games make us happy because they are hard work that we choose for ourselves, and it turns out nothing makes us happier than hard work." Yeah, it sounds weird, but if you think about it, you'll find it's true. Why do you enjoy playing golf? Wouldn't it be easier to just walk to the hole and gently drop your ball into it without the stress of using a metal club to hit it from hundreds of yards away? Yes, but there would be no challenge and thus no fun.

Brian Sutton-Smith, a psychologist who studies playing said, "The opposite of play isn't work. It's depression." The clinical definition of depression is "a pessimistic sense of inadequacy and despondent lack of activity." The opposite of depression would be

[97] https://venturebeat.com/2016/12/21/worldwide-game-industry-hits-91-billion-in-revenues-in-2016-with-mobile-the-clear-leader/
[98] http://www.hollywoodreporter.com/news/international-box-office-flatlines-2016-mpaa-report-says-987921

something like an optimistic sense of our own abilities and an invigorating rush of activity. If you think about it, that's exactly what play is.

A good game succeeds in activating all our brain and physical systems that underlie happiness: our attention system, our reward system, our motivation system, our emotions, and our memory systems. All of them are fully activated by a good game. No wonder they're addicting!

Jobs tend to be the opposite of games. We do them because we have to support ourselves. It can be demotivating because it comes with too much criticism and not enough praise; the consequences of failure might include not being able to pay our rent, and it might be repetitive and monotonous, especially at the entry level. Some jobs are also boring and leave us feeling underutilized, unappreciated, and as though we're wasting our lives. Also, in larger companies, it's hard to see how our work makes any difference. For Millennials, this is a double whammy since they were raised to follow their passions and change the world!

World of Warcraft (WOW) is probably the most popular online game in the world with 11 million players. WOW is beyond addicting in large part because the main focus is to constantly improve yourself (or more literally your character), and everybody loves doing that. You improve your avatar by earning points, and the more points you earn the more you get access to tougher challenges. This process is called "leveling up." There is always something to do to improve your character, and the challenges available to you are always just a little bit stronger than you are... enough to challenge you, but not so hard to make you feel defeated. On average, it takes a player 500 real world hours to develop their character to the maximum level. That's about a quarter of a year's worth of full time work, and most players have done it for more than one character. What could you get done in your company if you unlocked even a small fraction of that productivity?

So why are people spending so much time working on building characters in video games? There are many reasons, but one of the main ones is that good games give us clear missions and more satisfying work. Satisfying work means work that has a clear goal and actionable next steps. A clear goal but no next steps is stressful and more problematic than satisfying.

Games have a magical way of making failure fun. Gamers fail about 80% of the time that they attempt something new, but failure in the game is designed in such a way that it makes them feel excited, interested, and optimistic that they'll be able to do it next time.

If you're doubting whether gamification can create real motivation to get Millennials working hard in real-life, let us tell you about Chore Wars. It's an alternate reality game that you play in real-life. All quests involve getting real life cleaning chores done. It basically keeps track of all of the family members (or roommates) and helps inspire everyone to get more housework done. You get your roommates to sign up online and then you create custom adventures, like cleaning the kitchen, cleaning the toilet, and taking out the trash. When someone completes one of the chores, they log into the system and get points. The more points they get, the faster their avatar levels up. An exchange rate can even be set if you're playing with your kids, so they can exchange their earned points for an allowance. It sounds incredibly silly, but it works! If it can work for something as thankless as household chores, it can work for insurance work! Great gamification turns something that we have to do into something we want to do.

Games are such a powerful motivator that Tony rewarded himself for a successful 2016 by using his entire tax return to build a monster of a gaming computer, and he's rewarding himself for finishing this book by buying himself an Oculus Rift. If you don't know what that is, put the book down right now and go YouTube it! Better yet, find a nearby mall that has one on you can try yourself.

Chapter 24: Time to Embrace Transparency

Millennials are all about understanding the "why" behind corporate policies and have a hard time fitting in when they don't understand the reasoning. They have a strong preference for transparency and very little patience for corporate secrecy. It's a very human thing, just like candor and transparency produce trust between people, the same applies to the relationship between companies and their employees (and even their customers). Transparency produces trust, and that is a big win in the employer's relationship with employees. Secrecy damages trust. We love how Buffer explains it. "Transparency breeds trust, and trust is the foundation of great teamwork.[99]"

In our own industry, or rather at the InsurTech edges of our industry, Lemonade has been making waves with their Transparency Chronicles. Since their launch in late 2016, the world's most recognizable InsurTech company has written about transparency roughly once a month. Their first article, "Lemonade Launch Metrics Exposed," shared the "most interesting stats" from their first 48 hours as an active insurance company. They were very open, even about less than pretty parts, like the fact that their first day visitors had been overwhelmingly male (82.64%). They were even transparent about which companies people left to try Lemonade.

---

[99] Introducing Open Salaries at Buffer

At the end of their first quarter, they published a report being very honest about how the first few days of media fueled crazy growth, but things slowed down to a crawl short-term. They were also honest about the fact that 90% of their sales are renters insurance with only 10% being homeowners. They were honest that men still bought more than 75% of all policies they sold, and they didn't try to hide the fact that their customer service resolution time was well out of SLA for a few days in November. Our favorite part was the "What Didn't Work" part of the article where they fell on their sword and accepted the fact that they screwed up by calling their product Peer-to-Peer (P2P) insurance when it really wasn't that at all. They even included a screenshot of their checking account statement with Silicon Valley Bank. Can you imagine traditional insurance companies doing that?

We are not suggesting that every insurance company needs to become as transparent as Lemonade is, but they should at the very least be aware that that level of transparency is candy for Millennials. They simply do not understand the need for corporate secrecy. If their company is not misbehaving, then why would they be afraid of transparency? We know it's a hard shift, but it's one that will serve the industry well for the long-term.

Payscale, a compensation software company, did a study of 71,000 employees and found that one of the top predictors of employee engagement is a company's ability to communicate clearly about compensation. Open and honest discussion around pay was found to be more important than career development opportunities, and even enthusiasm for the company.

The study also found that very often people are wrong about how they're paid compared to the market. In fact, an incredible two-thirds of people who are paid at market rate think they're underpaid! Once you add that 60% of employees who think they are underpaid are wanting to leave their companies, you can see how not communicating openly about pay is costing your company a lot of unnecessary turnover.

Probably the most interesting thing the study found is that transparent conversations about pay can help keep employees engaged, even if they're paid below market rate. They found that 82% of employees paid below market, that worked for companies with very transparent pay structures, were still engaged. On the other side of that coin, they found that paying at the top of the market without being transparent was much less effective than if they were transparent about pay. Basically, they found no good reason to keep pay a secret. If you have the knowledge about market rate, and you choose to stay, you are staying for a reason. If you perceive that your company is hiding the fact that they pay less than market rate, you will feel duped. No one wants to work for a company that is trying to pull one over on them!

Gender also plays a role. Women who are paid above market are 18% more likely to believe they're underpaid than men, so pay transparency goes a long way towards helping you retain your high performing women.[100] Studies have found that unsurprisingly, pay transparency helps decrease the gender pay gap and pay discrimination[101].

Gallup has found that having real and transparent conversations with employees about pay structure and potential pay during interviews leads to much better engagement[102]. Studies by other organizations have shown that employees who are at least shown how their salary compares to others worked harder and increased their performance[103]. It makes perfect sense. An employee who can see a clear connection between how people that go above and beyond in the company get paid better will emulate their behavior. It makes it much easier for Millennials to figure out which behaviors and accomplishments a company values and rewards. For example, if a company really values field experience and CPCU, it will become obvious to their employees when they see that those are the characteristics the best paid people in each area share. They will know exactly what they need to do to grow

---

[100] Most People Have No Idea Whether They're Paid Fairly - HBR
[101] Pay Transparency - Penn State Law Review, Vol. 116, No. 4, p. 1043, 2012 by Gowri Ramachandran
[102] State of the American Workforce - Gallup
[103] Striving for Status

in the company. Other studies have found the same thing from the other side of the coin showing that salary secrecy decreases performance as pretty much everybody thinks they're underpaid and undervalued[104].

There are five levels of pay transparency[105]:

Level 1: Letting employees know they're allowed to discuss pay.

At this level you're just trying to break the social taboo prohibiting people talking about their pay.

Level 2: Publish pay scales or pay bands internally.

This is the level most large insurance companies are at. Pay bands are published internally with a range of pay for each band, and every job is transparently mapped to a band. It's a decent start, but it won't be enough for Millennials. Smaller carriers and agencies who don't have transparent pay bands should immediately start working towards getting to this level.

Level 3: Set a pay formula and disclose it.

---

[104] Signaling in Secret
[105] Why Being Transparent is Good for Business - WSJ

This is more of an alternative to transparency. The company sets a specific formula that takes into account role level, education, designations, tenure, and other characteristics to set a salary. Salaries aren't open, but if you have enough information about a coworker, you can calculate their salary. We have only heard of one carrier doing it this way. The disadvantages are that it lacks flexibility and can be manipulated, for example, people getting useless designations just to inflate their salary. It's better than level 1 (or level 0), but it's not ideal either.

Level 4: Internally transparent salaries.

Being completely transparent and internally publishing not only pay bands, but the actual exact salaries of all employees. Some companies also share performance data at the department, unit, or team level, but usually not at the individual level. We are not aware of a single insurance carrier that has transparent salaries at this point, but we can assure you it would go a *long* way towards engaging Millennials.

Level 5: Publically transparent salaries.

Making salaries transparent for everybody, not just internal employees, would be helpful in improving recruiting efforts and in improving our reputation in the overall economy. Buffer even has a Transparent Salary Calculator where a potential employee can figure out how much he or she would be paid if they got a job at Buffer! That's incredible. You can check it out here: https://buffer.com/salary.

As an industry, we need to transition towards getting every company to at least level 3 as soon as possible, and within the next few years. The more we move towards level 4, the better we'll be able to attract and retain Millennial talent.

Chapter 25: What about Gen Z?

It's hard to say exactly when the last Millennial was born. It depends on the demographer, but most put it somewhere between 1995 and 2000. If we go by David and Jonah Stillman's research and their resulting book, *Gen Z @ Work*, then the first Gen Zer was born in 1995. That would mean that the very first members of that generation will be graduating college and hitting orientation at your company at about the same time this book goes to print in 2017!

Yeah, that's right, our industry is just starting to get its head around what a majority Millennial workforce means for its very ingrained conservative attitudes, and we already have to start thinking about what the generation *after* the Millennials will demand. In other words, insurance companies are late to getting the Millennials right and have to start thinking about Gen Z already.

Carly and Tony are just starting their work on Gen Z, and this chapter is largely based on the excellent book mentioned in the first paragraph of this chapter by the father and son team of David and Jonah Stillman. This chapter will give you a summary of their work, but we highly recommend you read their book for the details. It's very interesting! We just wanted to make sure we at least gave you an intro to this new generation. In the rest of the book we source all numbers by footnotes, but in this chapter you can assume all numbers come from *Gen Z @ Work* unless otherwise specified.

In some ways, Gen Zers are hyper Millennials, but in other ways, they are very different, so you can't just treat them like Millennials. Most of those differences come because Gen Zers are not the kids of Baby Boomers, they're the kids of Gen Xers. Like Millennials, they are digital natives, to an even more extreme level, but unlike Millennials, they are less optimistic and more practical.

The Gen Zers were not only raised by skeptical Gen Xers, but they also grew up during the Great Recession of 2008 - 2012 and were deeply shaped by it. While the Millennials were raised by self-esteem boosting Baby Boomers, the Gen Zers were told by their parents that there are winners and there are losers in the world, and they were raised to be winners. They were raised to be competitive. The Gen Zers did get participation trophies, like the Millennials, but when they brought them home, their parents made it clear that winning is what really counts in life, and that even if you got a trophy for showing up, it doesn't mean anything unless you won. In other words, Gen Zers were raised with tough love. They are pragmatic, independent, and permanently stuck in survival mode.

Gen Zers have never known a world without smartphones and have never had to make do without 24/7 online connections. If online access is like water to the Millennials, it's like oxygen to the Gen Zers. This constant access to whatever information they want from anywhere in the world at their fingertips means they are an impatient generation that is going to have zero patience for what they will perceive as unnecessary corporate bureaucracy.

While Millennials (raised in a time of prosperity) are all about meaning in their work and making the world a better place, Gen Zers put money and security at the top of their priorities. That doesn't mean you can stop caring about the environment, ethics, and good corporate citizenship; they will punish you for that. Rather, it means that selling them on the social value of insurance needs to come second to selling them on what insurance can do for their long-term careers and how it is a stable career option. They do want to make a difference, but the psychological damage the Great Recession did to their psyche means their own financial security must be addressed first and foremost.

In some ways, they are hyper Millennials. Ninety-one percent of Gen Zers say that having the right technology is a big part of how they'll choose which companies to work for, so companies must redouble their efforts on improving their employee facing technology.

While Millennials are all about collaboration and will continue to demand teamwork, the Gen Zers are all about competition. They will get along well with competitive Boomers and skeptical Gen Xers, but they will appear too tech-obsessed and impatient. Millennials who are finally becoming managers will need to be trained on how to properly manage competitive, individualistic Gen Zers.

Chapter 26: Becoming a Talent Factory

At most large insurance carriers, it's fairly common to see managers, directors, and vice presidents getting moved around to different areas of the company, so they can become better rounded leaders. Unfortunately, as far as we have seen, this type of focus on development is much less common in the entry levels of the organization where most Millennials start their careers. There are some organizations, outside of the insurance industry, that are well-known for their extensive talent development programs at all levels of the company. Two such organizations are Procter & Gamble and HSBC Group. They were featured in a 2007 HBR article called "Make Your Company a Talent Factory." We will reference this extensively in this chapter.

HSBC instituted a system of local talent pools that track and manage the careers of high-potential employees within the firm, all the way down to the entry level. The high potential employees are placed in new assignments specifically designed to help them grow in exactly the dimensions where they need to grow and have interest in growing. Priority is given to cross-business unit projects that expose them to multiple areas.

Leaders are expected to keep close relationships with them, preferably face-to-face, and to address their development needs and concerns. The aim is to give them experiences that bring them a deep understanding of all aspects of the business. HSBC is very transparent in informing their high potential employees that advancement to top management requires experiences in at least two different areas.

One very interesting thing that HSBC does differently is their assessment of employees. They are not assessed on a numerical scale until they reach the top pools. Before that, all the feedback they receive is in terms of development needs and is very supportive. The whole idea is to get them to grow, not to stress them out with subjective numbers. The reward system is also built all the way to the top, to encourage business units and geographies to work together.

P&G has built a world-class global talent supply-chain through a process that's coordinated worldwide but executed locally. Hiring and promotions are handled by each local group, but high potential prospects and key stretch assignments are managed globally. As the prospects advance, each new job or project they are assigned to, has been ranked from "beginner" to "experienced" to make sure new prospects aren't burnt out and that experienced high potential employees aren't wasted on easy assignments.

A computerized system tracks all 135,000 employees with special emphasis on the 13,000 middle and upper management employees. The system also tracks succession planning at all levels, and even tracks diversity. Essentially, it makes talent visible at all levels, and P&G is ready to fill a difficult spot in a matter of days, if necessary. If P&G Japan all of the sudden needs a new Japanese-speaking manager for Crest with previous finance experience, the system can identify internal candidates best suited for the job very quickly.

The most amazing part is that the system even tracks the recruiting process, including recording interviews in detail with assessment of candidates and assigning scores using uniform criteria. The success rate of promotions is measured and a "lessons learned" review is done on all promotions that aren't successful. This extreme focus leads to 90+% success rates. An incredible 90% of their entry-level managers come straight from college and spend their entire careers at P&G.

Largely because of the extreme focus on talent management from the very entry levels, P&G's turnover rate is only 7.5%, including retirements. We would love to see insurance carriers figuring out ways to manage talent from the very beginning.

Imagine starting out as a customer service representative at an insurance call center. From the time you interviewed, your manager helped you visualize different career paths at the company. Whether your interest is in customer service management, product development, underwriting, sales management, claims, or loss control, your manager illustrated what each path looks like and the steps required to get there.

Every few months, your future path is discussed, and your progress to hit the required milestones to move in that direction is honestly assessed. You know exactly what you need to do, and Talent Development is working closely with you, so you always know which skills you should be focusing on, and they are always working on getting you on the right projects to stretch you in the areas you need to grow in.

At all times, you have an estimated time frame to when your next promotion is likely to happen and how you are doing in your progress towards it. This helps you always feel like you're making progress. During our hundreds of conversations with Millennials, the most common complaints we heard were, "I don't know how to grow from here," and "I feel like I'm stuck." A world-class talent management system would go a long way in retaining and engaging our Millennials, and it would help us be more effective in our overall business as our leaders became better rounded.

While becoming a talent factory will put you leaps and bounds in the right direction of retaining Millennials, it is just part of the whole picture. We leave you with one final example of an organization that has strived in creating a dynamic workplace for their Millennials.

César Salazar is a partner at 23 Design, a "Product Strategy and Design Studio," with offices in San Francisco and Mexico City. He wrote an awesome Medium article about how he made the most out of his Millennials, and we loved it! His approach is very different from anything we've seen in the insurance industry, and we think there's a lot that can be learned from his experiments.

Mr. Salazar makes it very clear that putting together a great team of Millennials is one of the hardest things he's ever done; he doesn't sugarcoat it!

César took an interesting approach. He discovered that the Millennials on his team *are* very competitive and *are* passionate about quality and the results of their work. They *are* willing to put in long hours, and they organize well around their leaders. But they demand an excellent leader to organize around, they don't just line up after poor managers. The key is to have an inspiring leader. They have no patience for bad leadership.

23 Design realized that the people they really wanted to hire didn't believe in hierarchies and wanted to work in "less authoritarian environments." So they tested different mechanisms with the express purpose of keeping the organization flat. They

have "no managers, no performance review, a simple organizational chart, no corner offices, and a friendly environment." We know this is a bit out there, but stay with us.

They decided that they would focus on creating a learning environment first and worry about productivity second. It worked! Not only was the team happy, it was also productive, and the clients were happy!

Since that worked, they went all in. They eliminated any language that divided them from the employees and declared the company a "Fellowship," and all members of the teams became "Fellows."

During interviews they realized that most designers they wanted to hire loved to travel but didn't travel a lot because of lack of vacation time. They weren't numbers people, so they didn't manage their money very efficiently. The company decided to start providing basic financial coaching to help the employees manage their personal finances better. Also, they made sure to provide more vacation time, up to 25 days per year. They started sponsoring a yearly two week trip with all the Fellows. The company pays transportation and accommodations, and the Fellows pay their meals, drinks, and entertainment. It costs them about $2,000 per employee each year, but it builds incredible loyalty to the company. Compare that to the cost of replacing an employee at more than $25,000 per employee that leaves.

Appendix A: References

Y Size Your Business by Jason Dorsey, seriously we stood on the shoulders of giants to write this book. Dorsey was the main one of those giants. We brought a lot of his concepts to insurance but to dig deeper into them go read *Y Size*. Of course, buy it from the InsNerds.com Bookshelf to help us develop more insurance content and write other books!

Manager Tools and Career Tools are amazing podcasts by long time executive coaches Mark Horstman and Mike Auzenne. They aim to produce timeless instead of timely content and it's presented topically in 30 minute podcasts. Regardless of what management or career issue you're dealing with, check in with Manager Tools! https://www.manager-tools.com/

You can learn more about adultolescents here: http://bigthink.com/think-tank/adultolescence-its-the-beginning-of-a-new-age

Great article about modern office design: https://www.bdcnetwork.com/workplace-design-trends-make-way-millennials

Pew Numbers on the Generations over time:
http://www.pewresearch.org/fact-tank/2016/04/25/millennials-overtake-baby-boomers/

6th International Business and Social Science Research Conference:
https://www.wbiconpro.com/452-Brian.pdf

Report on Existing Millennial Research - November 21, 2011 by The Griffith Insurance Education Foundation:
http://learn.valen.com/rs/331-LIT-031/images/Education%2BSummit%2BFindings%2BWhitepaper.pdf

Millennial Generation Attitudes About Work and the Insurance Industry 2012 by The Griffith Insurance Education Foundation and The Institutes: https://www.theinstitutes.org/doc/Millennial-Generation-Survey-Report.pdf

Building a Talent Magnet - How the Property and Casualty Insurance Industry Can Solve Its People Needs by McKinsey & Company:
http://www.aamga.org/files/hr/BuildingaTalentMagnet.pdf

Generational talent management for insurers - Strategies to attract and engage Generation Y in the US insurance industry by Deloitte:

http://www.griffithfoundation.org/uploads/Generational-talent-management-for-insurers.pdf

The Council of Economic Advisors. 15 Facts About Millennials. 2014: https://medium.com/@ObamaWhiteHouse/15-economic-facts-about-millennials-61ed355feeb3#.s1s0y0u3m

There's no job Millennial s won't leave: https://melmagazine.com/theres-no-job-millennials-won-t-leave-but-here-s-how-to-keep-them-a-bit-longer-312f45449126#.q2cg7t56d

Millennials should be the highest paid adults in American history: https://www.theatlantic.com/business/archive/2016/03/the-problem-with-millennials-pay/472011/

Center for American Progress: *When I Was Your Age - Millennials and the Generational Wage Gap:* https://www.americanprogress.org/issues/economy/reports/2016/03/03/131627/when-i-was-your-age/

Stop Complaining About Millennials. Hire the Best Ones and Win Big:

https://medium.com/design-thoughts-case-studies/stop-complaining-about-millennials-bring-the-best-ones-and-win-big-39b681b189be#.rui2uxy3k

Goldman Sach's Report on Millennials:
http://www.goldmansachs.com/our-thinking/pages/millennials/

The Millennial Impact Report 2015:
http://www.themillennialimpact.com/files/2015/07/2015-MillennialImpactReport.pdf

Stop Complaining about Millennials. Hire the Best Ones and Win Big:
https://medium.com/design-thoughts-case-studies/stop-complaining-about-millennials-bring-the-best-ones-and-win-big-39b681b189be#.iplgfu4nx

Millennials in Adulthood - Pew Research 2014:
http://www.pewsocialtrends.org/2014/03/07/millennials-in-adulthood/

Bureau of Labor Statistics - Insurance Underwriters 2015:
https://www.bls.gov/oes/current/oes132053.htm

8 Great Employee Benefits Millennials Actually Want:

http://workplace.care.com/8-great-employee-benefits-millennials-actually-want

This Year's Grads Will Job-Hop More Than Previous Grads?: https://blog.linkedin.com/2016/04/12/will-this-year_s-college-grads-job-hop-more-than-previous-grads

The Job Hopping Generation by Gallup: http://www.gallup.com/businessjournal/191459/millennials-job-hopping-generation.aspx

Amazon experiments with a 30 hour workweek: https://www.forbes.com/sites/timworstall/2016/08/28/amazons-experiment-with-a-30-hour-work-week-going-cruising-for-talent-among-women-with-children/#38dcd4751a08

Mind of the Millennial - Bentley University: http://www.bentley.edu/newsroom/latest-headlines/mind-of-millennial

Millennials Generation Go - Ernst & Young: http://www.ey.com/us/en/about-us/our-people-and-culture/ey-infographic-millennials-generation-go

For the first time living with parents edges out other living arrangements for 18-to-34 year olds - Pew:

http://www.pewsocialtrends.org/2016/05/24/for-first-time-in-modern-era-living-with-parents-edges-out-other-living-arrangements-for-18-to-34-year-olds/

Student Loan Aid Helps Employers Attract Millennials:
https://www.shrm.org/resourcesandtools/hr-topics/talent-acquisition/pages/student-loan-aid-attract-millennials.aspx

Employee Benefits: What each generation wants:
https://www.glassdoor.com/employers/blog/employee-benefits-what-each-generation-wants/

How each generation views employee benefits:
https://www.paychex.com/articles/hcm/infographic-generation-views-employee-benefits

How Millennials Want to Work and Live. Gallup:
http://www.gallup.com/reports/189830/millennials-work-live.aspx?utm_source=gbj&utm_medium=copy&utm_campaign=20160512-gbj

Millennials - The Next Generation of Business Owners:
https://www.xero.com/content/dam/xero/pdf/Millennial%20Small%20Business%20Owners%20Report.pdf

How Many Millennials Are Now Living At Home, Per State:

https://mba.millennialbusinessassociation.com/map-of-how-many-millennials-are-living-at-home-with-parents-in-each-us-state-2017-7ecbe595010c#.5i795d5vi

Millennials are now the biggest generation in the Canadian workforce:
http://www.canadianbusiness.com/innovation/the-millennial-majority-workforce/

70% of Millennial workers would rather telecommute than come to the office:
http://www.canadianbusiness.com/business-strategy/millennials-prefer-telecommuting/

A Generation of Leaders:
http://www.thehartford.com/sites/thehartford/files/millennial-leadership-2015.pdf

7 things the insurance industry needs to know about the looming talent gap:
http://www.propertycasualty360.com/2015/08/07/7-things-the-insurance-industry-needs-to-know-abou

2016 Insurance Industry Talent Trends:
https://jacobsononline.com/uploadfiles/leader296.pdf

The Impact of Student Loan Benefits on Your Employees:
https://www.sofi.com/benefits-whitepaper

The 2016 Deloitte Millennial Survey - Winning over the next
generation of leaders:
https://www2.deloitte.com/content/dam/Deloitte/global/Documen
ts/About-Deloitte/gx-millenial-survey-2016-exec-summary.pdf

Gallup - State of the American Workforce:
http://www.gallup.com/reports/199961/state-american-workplace-
report-2017.aspx

Understanding Millennials - Millennial Mindset:
https://millennialmindset.co.uk/understanding-millennials/

PWC Top Issues: The Aging Workforce
http://www.pwc.com/us/en/insurance/publications/assets/pwc-
insurance-top-issues-aging-workforce.pdf

Accenture: The insurance workforce of the future:
https://www.accenture.com/us-en/insight-insurance-workforce-of-
the-future

Deloitte: Human capital trends in the insurance industry:
https://www2.deloitte.com/content/dam/Deloitte/us/Documents/st

rategy/us-cons-human-capital-trends-in-the-insurance-industry.pdf

HBR: Make your company a talent factory:
https://hbr.org/2007/06/make-your-company-a-talent-factory

Reinventing Performance Management:
https://hbr.org/2015/04/reinventing-performance-management

Deloitte - How Insurance Companies Can Beat The Talent Crisis:
http://www.griffithfoundation.org/uploads/Deloitte-on-Ins-Talent-Crisis.pdf

Talent Crisis Remains a Challenge:
http://riskandinsurance.com/talent-crisis-remains-challenge/

Insurance Industry Rethinking Recruitment Strategies:
http://www.insurancejournal.com/news/national/2017/01/27/440212.htm

The Hartford - 2014 Millennials Leadership Survey:
http://www.thehartford.com/sites/thehartford/files/millennial-leadership.PDF

The Hartford - Millennial Research-at-a-Glance:
https://www.thehartford.com/resources/gb/millennial-research

Solving the Insurance Industry Talent Crisis by Investing in Risk Management and Insurance Graduates - IRMI Insights: https://www.irmi.com/docs/default-source/authoritative-reports/insights/insurance-industry-talent-recruiting.pdf

Move Over Gen Y, Gen Z is here: https://blog.hrps.org/blogpost/Move-Over-Millennials-Gen-Z-Is-Here

Improving Perceptions of the Insurance Industry The Influence of Insurance Professionals - Risk Management and Insurance Review, 2016, Vol. 19, No. 1, p 147-166. http://onlinelibrary.wiley.com/doi/10.1111/rmir.12058/abstract

Why you should know how much your co-workers get paid: https://ideas-ted-com.cdn.ampproject.org/c/ideas.ted.com/why-you-should-know-how-much-your-coworkers-get-paid/amp/

USAA raises minimum wage and adds 12 weeks of parental leave for both moms and dads: http://www.mysanantonio.com/business/local/article/USAA-sets-16-minimum-wage-adds-parent-benefit-11065782.php#photo-12354724

The 2017 Insurance Industry Employment and Hiring Outlook Survey:
http://images.greatinsurancejobs.com/pdfs/gij-whitepaper/2017_Great_Insurance_Jobs_Insurance_Industry_Employment_Outlook.pdf

Why being transparent about pay is good for business:
https://www.wsj.com/articles/why-being-transparent-about-pay-is-good-for-business-1464660062

Striving for Status: A Field Experiment on Relative Earnings and Labor Supply:
http://econgrads.berkeley.edu/emilianohuet-vaughn/files/2012/11/JMP_e.pdf

Signaling in Secret: Pay for Performance and the Incentive and Sorting Effects of Pay Secrecy:
http://amj.aom.org/content/57/6/1706.abstract

Pay Transparency:
https://papers.ssrn.com/sol3/papers.cfm?abstract_id=1925604

Pay Secrecy and Wage Discrimination:
https://iwpr.org/publications/pay-secrecy-and-wage-discrimination/

Move Over 401ks: This New Perk Helps Millennials Pay Off
College Loans:
https://www.usnews.com/news/articles/2016-04-18/move-over-
401-k-s-this-new-perk-helps-millennials-pay-off-college-loans

Student Debt Viewed as Major Problem; Financial Considerations
Important Factor for Most Millennials When Considering Whether
to Pursue College:
http://iop.harvard.edu/student-debt-viewed-major-problem-
financial-considerations-important-factor-most-millennials-when

New America - Policy Brief The Student Loan Debt Review -
February 2014:
https://s3.amazonaws.com/www.newamerica.org/downloads/The
StudentDebtReview_2_18_14.pdf

Student Loan Repayment Could be 2017's Hottest Employee
Benefit:
http://time.com/money/4569867/student-loan-repayment-
employee-benefit/

Life Delayed: The Impact of Student Debt on the Daily Lives of
Young Americas:
http://www.asa.org/site/assets/files/4743/life_delayed_whitepaper
_2015.pdf

Your Employer Might Help Pay Off Your Student Loans:
http://time.com/money/4555841/student-loans-employer-benefit/

These Companies Help Pay Off Their Employees' Student Loan Debt:
http://time.com/money/4261054/employee-student-loan-repayment-programs/

Are Student Loan Repayment Plans The Next Big Employee Benefit?:
https://www.forbes.com/sites/kellypeeler1/2016/08/01/are-student-loan-repayment-plans-the-next-big-employee-benefit/#8250d171f94a

Student Loan Assistance: It attracts Millennial talent & keeps them in their seats:
https://www.hr.com/en/topleaders/all_articles/student-loan-assistance-it-attracts-millennial-tal_it903tke.html

Survey Finds Student Loan Reimbursement a Hot New Benefit for Job Seekers:
https://www.businesswire.com/news/home/20160201005086/en/Survey-Finds-Student-Loan-Reimbursement-Hot-Benefit

The Key to Attracting Millennials:

http://www.edassist.com/resources/research-reports-webinars/millennials-study-executive-report

Medical, Dental, 401(k)? Now Add School Loan Aid to Job Benefits:
https://www.nytimes.com/2016/03/26/your-money/medical-dental-401-k-now-add-school-loan-aid-to-job-benefits.html?_r=4

The Latest Job Benefit: Paying Employees' Student Loans:
http://fortune.com/2016/05/18/job-benefit-paying-employees-loans/

More Than 40% of Student Borrowers Aren't Making Payments:
https://www.wsj.com/articles/more-than-40-of-student-borrowers-arent-making-payments-1459971348

More Companies Help Employees Pay Off Student Loans:
https://www.wsj.com/articles/more-companies-help-employees-pay-off-student-loans-1459130781

4 reasons why employers should offer student loan repayment aid as a perk:
http://www.bizjournals.com/bizjournals/how-to/human-resources/2016/03/student-loan-repayment-aid-as-a-perk.html?page=all

The Hartford Launches Apprenticeship Program To Prepare Students For Careers In Insurance:
https://newsroom.thehartford.com/releases/the-hartford-launches-apprenticeship-program-to-prepare-students-for-careers-in-insurance?cmp=SOC-BRA-HartBeat-21771816

Debt relief could be the next big perk:
http://herald-review.com/business/investment/debt-relief-could-be-the-next-big-perk/article_11818536-8642-5af6-bdb5-0213d4aae440.html

The Disproportionate Burden of Student-Loan Debt on Minorities:
https://www.theatlantic.com/education/archive/2015/05/the-disproportionate-burden-of-student-loan-debt-on-minorities/392456/

Jet Blue's Stay-At-Home Work Force:
http://www.cbsnews.com/news/jet-blues-stay-at-home-work-force/

How to Hire a Millennial:
https://www.financial-planning.com/news/how-to-hire-a-millennial

Difference Between Internship & Apprenticeship:

http://work.chron.com/difference-between-internship-apprenticeship-29606.html

Most People Have No Idea Whether They're Paid Fairly:
https://hbr.org/2015/10/most-people-have-no-idea-whether-theyre-paid-fairly

Why a Transparent Culture is Good For Business:
https://www.fastcompany.com/3036794/why-a-transparent-culture-is-good-for-business

Introducing Open Salaries at Buffer: Our Transparent Formula and All Individual Salaries:
https://open.buffer.com/introducing-open-salaries-at-buffer-including-our-transparent-formula-and-all-individual-salaries/

10 Things Entrepreneurs Need to Know About Intrapreneurship:
https://www.inc.com/murray-newlands/10-things-entrepreneurs-need-to-know-about-intrapreneurship.html

The 4 Essential Traits of Intrapreneurs:
https://www.forbes.com/sites/davidkwilliams/2013/10/30/the-4-essential-traits-of-intrapreneurs/#472ca74d51da

Unhappy at Work? Be an Intrapreneur:

https://www.wired.com/insights/2013/05/unhappy-at-work-be-an-intrapreneur/

The Rise of the Intrapreneur:
https://www.fastcompany.com/3046231/the-rise-of-the-intrapreneur

Big Companies That Embrace Intrapreneurship Will Thrive:
https://www.entrepreneur.com/article/243884

Lesson #135: Why Big Companies Struggle with Innovation:
http://redrocketvc.blogspot.com/2013/02/lesson-135-why-big-companies-struggle.html

8 Ways to Effectively Lead Entrepreneurial Employees:
https://www.entrepreneur.com/article/236433

Millennials are the True Entrepreneur Generation:
https://www.forbes.com/sites/robasghar/2014/11/11/study-millennials-are-the-true-entrepreneur-generation/#3c958ea73dc4

Why Millennials Could Be The Most Entrepreneurial Generation Ever:
https://www.americanexpress.com/us/small-business/openforum/articles/why-millennials-could-be-the-most-entrepreneurial-generation-ever/

PC360 What it takes to attract and keep insurance & financial service employees:
http://www.propertycasualty360.com/2017/05/18/what-it-takes-to-attract-and-keep-insurance-finan?page_all=1&slreturn=1495466250

Acknowledgements

This book would not have been possible without the contributions of many people. Because of lack of space here, I will name just a few. My partner-in-crime, Carly Burnham, who is the brain behind InsNerds and all of our projects together. Andrew Holland, who was always my tireless sounding board as we walked the Skywalk in Des Moines for hours on end during our time at Nationwide. Dan Behrens and Kyle Cropp who hired me into the Farm Bureau Express Claims team, my first job in the industry that I fell in love with. Kristy Olson, and the rest of the Farm Bureau HR and Training team, who ignited my interest in insurance and my addiction to insurance education. Jason Latham, Eric Tharpe, and Sandra Matarrese-Keeling who changed my career forever, taking a risk in putting me through the FLRP Program at Nationwide, and who gave me career changing, honest, tough love, and great feedback. Michael Koscielny, Lamong Boyd, Dale Halon, Rob Galbraith, Rich Pudleiner, Perry Trowbridge, Rodney Wilson, Ramya Sunad, Chris Hampshire, Adam Haugerud, Danielle Baker, Elaine George, Michael Shneibaum, Bruce Hicks, Mike Holms, Sandra Masters, Brian Schmidt, Leah Heller, Hema Chaurasia, Kylie Jones, Greg Deimling, Joan Fitzsimmons, Melissa Stream, John Masselli, Brian Gerritsen, Cindy Baroway, Theresa Fabela, and the many hundreds of fellow CPCUs at the CPCU Society who debated with me during Annual Meetings, Leadership Summits, Local Chapter

Meetings, New Designee Committee LME Interest Group, and on the CPCU Candidates Group on Facebook. Abe Kane, Joe Ferrone, Josh Pestano, Jessie Robinson, Chris Stultz, Rachel Banister, Megan Whittemore, Ada Hoffer-Perkins, Arthur Gray, Julian Banchon, and the rest of the young lifers who keep coming back year after year, many without employer support. Jon Pyle who opened my eyes to the possibility of looking beyond claims for the right opportunities. Deb Miller, Michaela Goen, and the rest of the crew at 1100 Toastmasters who taught me to slow down and to be a much better speaker. Dick Clinard who taught me that the biggest thing I could do is help others grow their careers. Ted Lussem who taught me that if you do a little bit every day, people start to think you've done a lot.

Tony

~~~

I will echo Tony in saying this book is made possible due to the support of many. Firstly, Tony, without his crazy ideas, passion, and drive, I would never have considered a book on this subject. Bonnie Perkins gave me my first job in the insurance industry as a CSR at her insurance agency. I was fortunate to start my journey in insurance learning from an agent who truly believed in the mission of insurance. She was a fantastic role model and teacher. In addition, I am grateful for the support many of my fellow

CPCUs, including Rob Galbraith, Greg Massey, and Lamont Boyd. Finally, I am thankful to many at Erie Insurance who have cemented my belief that insurance companies are fantastic places to work and be challenged. In particular, I would not have had the experiences at Erie Insurance that I've had without Jeff Graml, who was a fantastic trainer and who encouraged me from the beginning of my time there to push myself and give back to the company and the industry through National CPCU Society Service. I am grateful to all of my mentors, managers, and fellow employees at Erie Insurance who truly follow our founder's instruction to "Think." I will carry this reminder with me throughout my career.

Carly

About the Authors

Carly Burnham

Carly began her insurance career in 2004 as an office assistant at an agency in her hometown of Duluth, MN. She got licensed as a producer while working at that agency and progressed to serve as an office manager. Working in the agency is how she fell in love with the industry. She saw firsthand the good that insurance consumers experienced by having the proper protection.

When Carly moved to Des Moines in 2010, she decided to commit to the industry, and she completed her CPCU in one year, finishing it in 2012 and attending commencement in New Orleans. She completed her MBA at Iowa State University in 2014. During this time, she and Tony founded a Gen Y Associate Resource Group at Nationwide in Des Moines.

After they both left Nationwide, Tony recruited Carly to co-author and manage InsNerds.com. She has the difficult task of keeping his constant flow of crazy ideas focused and helping to flesh them out into useful articles. Carly enjoys sharing knowledge and ideas about the future of the industry and finds the website a good outlet for this passion.

Carly is currently a Commercial Underwriter at Erie Insurance, in

Erie, PA. She is involved in the Presque Isle CPCU Society Chapter; the CPCU Society New Designee Committee; the CPCU Society Underwriting Interest Group; the CPCU Society Leadership and Managerial Excellence Interest Group; and the Commercial Underwriting Training Program at Erie Insurance. She also writes "Next Wave," a monthly column in the "Perspectives" section of Best's Review.

You can view more about her on her Linkedin Profile: https://www.linkedin.com/in/carlyburnham/

Tony Cañas

Tony Cañas is a young insurance nerd, blogger, podcaster, and speaker. He's the voice of the Millennial generation in the insurance industry, helping the industry understand how to engage this large demographic that will soon make up over 50% of the workforce.

Tony was born and raised in Costa Rica and moved to the US in 2002, receiving his BS in Management Information Systems and MBA both from Iowa State University. He has been in the insurance industry since 2009. During that time he has completed his CPCU, AU, AIC, ARM, ARe, ASLI, API, AIS and AINS designations along with his Toastmaster's Competent Communicator and Advanced Communicator Bronze public speaking designations. Having worked in claims, underwriting, finance, and sales at four different insurance carriers, six cities, and five states, he has gained a broad understanding of the industry.

Tony has been very involved in the industry's effort to recruit and retain Millennials and has become a well known speaker and blogger on the topic.

Tony's favorite activity in the world is presenting his one hour session about Engaging and Retaining Millennials in the Insurance Industry. Tony shows up in his superman shirt, red sports jacket, and red shades and entertains and informs the audience in this unique-in-the-industry interactive experience. On average, 80% of the audience rates the presentation as "Very Good" or "Excellent" in the live survey at the conclusion.

In the last few years, he has presented it at the CPCU Society Leadership Conference in Phoenix; the CPCU Society Annual Meeting in Anaheim; the Ohio Insurance Education Day in Columbus; RISC Trends in Richmond, Virginia; the NAMIC Personal Lines Conference in Chicago; and in a variety of local CPCU Society Chapters.

He has been featured by "The Edge," the national magazine of the CPCU Society; the newsletter of the Iowa CPCU Society;

American Agent & Broker; and was named as one of the "Top Young Agents of 2013" by PropertyCasualty360.

Tony is passionate about insurance, technology, innovation, and about engaging Millennials in the insurance industry.

You can view more about him on his Linkedin Profile: https://www.linkedin.com/in/tonycanas/

CPSIA information can be obtained
at www.ICGtesting.com
Printed in the USA
LVOW13s1736070817
544123LV00036B/1528/P

9 781547 131105